Essays From The Couch

Volume IV...Et Cetera

WILLIAM S. HOROWITZ M.D.

ISBN: 1502545187

ISBN 13: 9781502545183

This collection is dedicated to the memory of
Peggy Sr., Mimi, and Rob, all of whom left before their
time and are sorely missed.

ACKNOWLEDGMENTS

I am totally in debt to my helpful wife, Gloria Jean, for sustaining me, enabling me to write. Too, our talks have often provided the stimulation for new ideas to develop. My son Nicholas, Philip Bronner, M.D. and Kelly Talbot have all shepherded this work into print, for which I am most grateful. My family, colleagues, friends and patients have all played a significant role in addition. I conceive of these collected works as my legacy and tribute to my and Gloria's families.

MISSION STATEMENT:

Both the 19th Century Freud and his 20th Century disciple confirm the wisdom of their historic predecessor: "And the truth shall set you free."

But that emancipation is not easily achieved, for adult man still wrestles with the shackles of ancient indoctrination, presented by the clerics as guidance but effecting instead his obedience. The transmission of values and conduct is valuable; the powerful inhibition of man thinking for himself is what is crippling.

The sharing of his unique mental life with an understanding companion re-establishes that original nurturing bond with another which releases the inherent growth of the self and its own thinking, an actual, not metaphorical, re-birth.

TABLE OF CONTENTS

AMERICAN *EXCEPTIONALISM*

William S. Horowitz, M.D.
September 11, 2013

Today the air is filled with patriotic themes, a product of this sad/ proud anniversary of the major attack on this country and its courageous response. Perhaps it would be timely to take this occasion to go beyond Charles Krauthammer, M.D.'s outstanding mastery of political history to explore the individual psychology he so assiduously avoids,,,.. "I'm not acting as a psychiatrist here".

The term *Exceptionalism* taken literally is obviously true, our form of government being consciously modeled as different from all others then extant. There is no argument here. It is the loading of the term with emotional meaning in order to persuade others (exerting political influence) that deserves scrutiny.

To claim that America was exceptionally open, unassuming, helpful, optimistic, receptive and naïvely trusting with much to learn, seemed fair and inoffensive enough. To load the term with a superlative inference begins to provoke offense to other countries which certainly believe they are just as powerful, moral, righteous, justified in existing, and caring for its people as we are. To take credit for worthy international deeds, to accept acknowledgements and honors for them is one thing; to infer superiority is quite another. The egoist is universally scorned; modest strength is not only respected but powerfully effective. People(s) can accept their betters, even assume them, but not their own inferiority.

Has the United States provoked envy, hostility, and a spoiling urge amongst other nations at times (as "the world's only superpower")? Whether justified or not, is it important to perceive, evaluate, and consider in our actions? Absolutely! Is it something to control our national behavior? Absolutely not! The statesman expresses quiet determination while recognizing it does not suit his objective to arouse unnecessary resistance; the politico seeking prominence with his proposal thinks "the brasher the better".

Is there room for *others* in our world view? If so, does an alliance with one detract from us, or our ability to "do business" with even more? We made common cause with Communist Russia during WWII to defeat Hitler, and even paid a half-century getting over it in the "Cold War" that followed. Now secular Russia is proposing an alliance of sorts with Syria and us to resist the march of the Islamic Brotherhood, which they equally abhor...but we seem to keep them as the hostile enemy, forgetting past history. *Collaboration* may offer a solution.

Now, *there's* a word with an antithetical meaning. Collaboration in WWII meant trading with the enemy, ala Quisling, to save your own skin. Keith Ablow, M.D. has suggested It is a variant of this "Stockholm Syndrome", practiced by arch exemplar George Soros giving up the Jews in Nazi days, and his contemporary puppet Barach Obama, who are engineering the decline of our culture in the face of the Moslem onslaught! That would make him not a feared super-power behind the scenes, but merely a familiar scared Patty Hearst in drag. Now *there's* a powerful idea from a fellow psychiatrist!

Perhaps we students of the mind have a place in contemporary discourse after all. People, as we all are, have experience with their own operations as well as such are intuitive experts about the operations of larger collections of people. It is the wisdom of the people which our "Fathers" empowered in our new nation, after all, and we would do well to exercise it. One of the lessons learned might be that politics, the art of exerting power over others, might be to resist rather than respect its influence on our own native thinking as those between them and others, and

JUSTICE

William S. Horowitz, M.D.
August 3, 2013

The mechanical T.V. spokesman announces today's news: "Picked up this morning is this [unshaven 35 year old] wearing an electronic ankle bracelet because of overcrowded jail, out on bail awaiting trial for raping a woman, apprehended after raping another woman."

I can see it now with my only slightly beclouded glasses: after a many- week to a year wait, he will be tried, convicted, and sentenced to 10, 20, (maybe even 100 years in the case of undue indignation) back into the jammed jail as his "punishment".

Would some sympathetic soul out there _pleeze_ enlighten me.... WHERE IS THE JUSTICE ? Is there some satisfaction forthcoming to the TWO victims ? Not likely, more likely _bitterness_ at the indifference of her fellow man to her. How about the other good women witnessing this as they hide their daughters behind their skirts. Shouts of pleasure? Not likely. How about the citizens at large in this society ? Are they feeling accomplished at the jails brimming over, never wondering what attracts so many to this system of "justice"? I wondered, but no more; it has utterly failed as a deterrent, maybe even functions as an attractant, lowering the cost of criminal activity and thereby raising the reward.

To the judges, believing they are performing an important social function, as their calendar now stretches into _years ahead?_ Not apparently, as their office hours stretch all the way from mid-morning to mid-afternoon, leaving ample time for "consideration, advisement", and decision-making. To the lawyers? Well, it's a living. As satisfying or not as it may be, there is no denying they perform a social function something like the street-sweepers of the 1800-'s. Is that JUSTICE? Or house-cleaning of the mess in its absence?

In the "olden days" on the frontier of this young nation (I have a *long* memory), they didn't have overcrowded jails, or communities over-run with rapists and murderers. When they caught a relatively ordinary criminal stealing someone else's horse, they held a "trial" at the nearest tall tree and strung him up, and dry-washed their hands in satisfaction afterwards. To my un-modern, un-sophisticated, un-sympathetic mind, THAT WAS JUSTICE !

What, who have changed this? The so-called "bleeding hearts? Our reaching for *ideals ?* Our losing touch with the hard feel of *reality ?* An admired English tradition of good manners ? Christian "tolerance" ?_Our "getting by", complacency, successful survival ? Is that success to be our undoing? What a damned shame if that is the case.

Indian Braves learn in the school of Mother Nature for that is what they have to deal with, having little or nothing beclouding between them. Now, *we* have thermostatically heated homes, but has Nature changed, specifically *human* nature? Obviously not. Are some people out to capture us, control us, "scalp" us? Does the weather care if it floods us, dries our fields, terrifies us with its storms? Do we think we have conquered Nature with our inventions and products? When we tell Jose that what he is doing is "against the law" (another one of our inventions), do we think he is listening, understanding, caring what another is thinking?

Now it is no longer necessary for each of us to grow our own corn, but possessing heaps of it loose in open public display should alert us to the fact that residents of neighboring communities may not have any and covet what we do....(which even the Brave would understand). Simple realities are quite sufficient to adjudge and dispose of *criminal* (asocial) acts. Gradations of heinous (totally unacceptable) behavior serve absolutely no purpose but legal employment and psychological curiosity. It would be perfectly efficient to have a jury trial to adjudge whether the act, including *all* degrees of killing, were justified or not in the opinion of the jury of peers ("would *they* do it?). *That* would produce "justice": quick, cheap, and deterrent punishment. Culpability is no arcane legalism but a simple human judgment. Our legal system, and its community sponsor, could take a lesson from any ordinary business, athletic team, or military unit about prompt elimination of members who don't fit in.

To the extent we pursue actual practices of IN-justice, to that extent we reap an UN-just society, such as we are suffering today.

THE UNREALITY OF REALITY?

William S. Horowitz, M.D.
September 21, 2013
With a bow to Sartre and Gloria

It is Saturday morning, and there is nothing to do but to contemplate one's existence, n'est ces pah? Fortunately, my wife is eager to have the subject taken up since she has pondered on it since early childhood, having been raised in an environment of constant change and isolation which rendered her traumatized. Having a like soul as companion saved the day for me from certain oblivion!

Trying to define *reality* as what is happening now is impossible because it is constantly changing...i.e., there is no _now_ now, to quote Stein. If what is real is in a constant state of flux, then does it only become real when it no longer lives? What is alive is not real; what is dead is real? A man can only be _really_ known in his biography (which perforce suffers from incompleteness)?

If all existence is unreal, an only-apparent experience seeming real, then what is the point of going on, and even worse, making _new_ life? _THAT_ is her question. Indeed, it takes a philosopher to answer it. Now, the psychiatrists have a word for it: they call a process of perceiving the real as unreal as _derealization,_ robbing it of meaning for psychological reasons. This seeming simple name change actually shifts the phenomenon from the actual to the perceptual to the motivational significance of it, an operation that can promise not only understanding but doing something about it.

Why would someone do this, deny the reality of an experience? _PAIN,_ of which we have 57 varieties. It hurts! How much? More than I'm afraid I can bear. Which is worse...fear, or blank, not knowing the people and places you have known, the actual life you have lived, the totality of your life or a disturbing realization of a part of it? YOU decide, you choose, which portion to erase. Given the conscious choice rather than a reflexive automatic one, perhaps you will recover pleasant memories of the joys you've been missing.

Now that we have solved that puzzle, let's move on to the meaning of existence, the actual significance of reality. We say that is real which is detected by any of our five sense organs, evolved for that very purpose. O.K., but what about my love for my wife...isn't that real, too?

And my contempt for Obama? Those are emotions...we _do feel_ them, too. What about ideas, like ambitions, plans, goals? We _look_ to them to guide us on the path we cannot yet see. They are _mental_ signals, no less perceived inside than outside. And they are real, too.

Intellectually, one can argue real is not really real, which maybe an exercise in Sophistry, but in the real world, it seems to be. Count on it!

"YOU'RE DRIVING ME CRAZY!"

William and Gloria Horowitz
October 7, 2013

Ever heard that? Of course, a commonality...but does it really happen, or is it just hyperbole? I think it does, and is well worth illuminating.

First of all, it happens between two people in contention who know each other, who _care_. It is an attempt at conflict resolution that leads to impotent paralyzing rage, most unpleasant to the target, of blithe unimportance to the "innocent" perpetrator. That contrast by itself is highly provocative of the rage reaction which ensues.

The mechanism of inducing this reaction is relatively simple, by presenting two conflicting, incompatible ideas, feelings, actions which cannot be reconciled with each other and leave the target "nonplussed", paralyzed, impotent of a response, which then leaves him enraged and impelled to act out. One could speculate that this sequence is not rare in cases of domestic violence.

The idea of impotizing powerful adults is irresistibly attractive to children, and the whole _"ploy"_ is reminiscent of those operations. In addition, the child plays "innocent" professionally, thereby not only defeating his opponent but humiliating him in the process. It is David and Goliath right at home. Certain adults practice this same infuriating logic in their arguments, stereotypically "dumb blondes".

Where to suspect this is operating in one of your cases? When the subject repetitiously engages in offensive behavior never seeming to learn or correct his "errors", whilst otherwise exhibiting commonplace intelligence. He will probably be experienced more as a pest that an evil-doer, and be quickly forgiven (which he acts like he expects). Far from innocent, this behavior is highly maladaptive and fixating to psychological development. It is childish mischief writ large.

Amazing that something so simple could trip someone up for life.

THOUGHTS

William S. Horowitz, M.D.
December 14, 2013

I am thinking, and what a wonderful feeling that is, to be thinking. Do you also feel that? I am realizing, remembering the corner of Murray Avenue and Capitol Drive where we lived at 3548 N. Murray Avenue, Shorewood, remembering how *belonging* I felt. I was a *part* of it. I didn't know then to credit my father for *belonging,* for he totally abjured the hyphen. My mother, dear one, felt I was missing something, and insisted I make myself a JEWISH-AMERICAN by being confirmed in that group. So I did, at 16, being a "good boy", and proceeded to feel only half-belonging there, both as an American and as a Jew. That adds up to *nowhere, or nobody,* you see.

Is that the problem of Jews? Do they feel unaffiliated, unidentified? Is that why they proclaim their presence, and importance, loudly in every gathering of miscellany? *BECAUSE THEY FEEL LIKE NOBODY?* Is this what Chaim Weitzman realized ? They needed a homeland to feel legitimized ? And in fact, that homeland has delivered that expectation in spades: nobody fools around with a SABRA !

What a thought! The "invention" of the Jews by some ancient cult founders proclaiming their "special" attributes actually <u>wiped them out</u> !!! All these good people down through the ages with their accumulated in-breeding and consequent intelligence have felt like non-members of the human race, aliens so to speak, harvesting the universal opprobrium awarded to the *outsider, and feeling like nothing to boot !* THAT is why certain classical authors (Jay Gonen at al.) have called Judaism a *curse*). And it is why I proclaim the ancient rabbinate <u>*TRAITORS*</u>.

Shlomo Sands recent research on the purported continuity of the Jewish tribe for thousands of years has put a lie to it, characterizing it only as a religion serially adopted and rejected by miscellaneous population groups down through the ages. Reading his work had the almost magical effect of "liberating" me from an unknown restraint, for which I am most grateful and am enthusiastically recommending it to others. You have no idea how good it feels to be whole ! (Because you were unaware you had a jacket on you.)

Fast forward to today, brown faces loudly proclaiming their *"rights"* all over TV, ad nauseam. Rights to what? What is mine, my heritage, Shakespeare? No, they have no "rights" beyond those of everyone else...to be themselves. THAT means *being* themselves, and not somebody (or 1/2 somebody) else. African-Americans are NOBODY, got it? You are railing against your own living arrangements. Follow the Jews out of your historic poor neighborhoods into the sun. Establish your place in the sun! Be somebody and you will be regarded as somebody. It starts with you, dummy...not me.

A psychiatrist (who's dat?) might opine that the world is suffering from an identity disorder, nobody knowing who they are. "Globalization, One-Worldness?" Why izzat? Why, that's the message of the masses, those without achievement but wanting what YOU have. They even call themselves "THE PEOPLE"! The nerve of them, speaking in the name of all of us! Well, I for one am not "one of the demos", declaring myself one apart, an individual, my own man. Where did the rest of you drop that pride and self-respect? Is that blasphemous? Or is that divine?

THE ASSAULT ON THE ENGLISH LANGUAGE

William S. Horowitz, M.D.
December 15, 2013

LOL, Buymenow, M.I.5: what do *you* call it? It is communication to be sure, transmitting information, often in disguise but hardly a language. "Evolving" speech patterns in the modern technology culture? "Overnight" seems more apt than *evolving*.

Chaucer will be turning over in his grave witnessing the dissolution of his language, but he is not alone. Ask any American adult past the age of consent and he will tell you he cannot decipher what his own children are saying. So, is it an "age thing"? Eagerly adopted by the young, certainly, but invented by them? One suspects not.

A recent informational brochure delivered by my local hospital listed the names of the current physician staff, which consisted of 300 pictures with foreign names, of which *only ONE was an American!* What are they doing here? What are they speaking? To enable the native workforce to be replaced by foreign-speaking immigrants is no trick for a purposeful economic policy, which neatly weakens the language and the culture with the same stone. It seems a surreptitious invasion has taken place beneath our very noses with the welcoming of all comers. And this is only the beginning of the second term of our present administration!

There are at least three popular forms of "NEWSPEAK" now appearing: the ever popular "TEXTING" or use of abbreviations or single letters (charged by the letter); eliminating spaces in phrases or sentences so words run together; or coded messages, numbers, letters, symbols preferred by the police and military. The least obvious and most insidious, however, is the gradual elimination of *"NEWS"* itself, whether by newspaper, radio or television broadcast, magazines, etc, which are going out of business serially. Reliable "old-school" reporters have analyzed the bulk of what is still offered as news these days is pure political narrative (story-telling for persuasive effect) or propaganda.

You, we, are being *cultivated*, cannily and contemptuously by the political power which captured control of our country, silently robbed of our personhood. Why us? Because unspoken but generally recognized, "Western" Civilization has reached its apogee in the English-speaking (synonymous with *white*) *world*, and is the envy and target of every third-rate culture trailing badly. Soon, you will be unable to speak or listen to anyone not authorized. Have you noticed the spate of "speech infractions"(and retractions) lately by the TV anchors?To you dummies (rhymes with *demos*) who still "believe", you deserve every fate which awaits you. I am leaving shortly.

AGENCY

William S. Horowitz, M.D.
January 22, 2014
Revised

Wha? What are you referring to? The agency is the actor, the do-er of the action, the one who carries out the action and receives the attendant credit or blame for it. We are considering today the ins and outs of carrying out actions and their implications.

Perhaps the most important of these issues is that of _responsibility,_ the bearing of that credit or blame. Intuitively, we know there is a correlation between that ability and the age of the bearer, and the younger the do-er, the more ludicrous his disclaimers become. But do we also conclude the opposite is true: that the assumption of authorship is a faithful measure of maturity, of responsibility, _adulthood_? Or is it ? Perhaps it is not a fixed relationship but a relative _one, credit or blame depending on one's frame of reference, one's value_ system.

So we can have a blood-thirsty Arab claiming _credit_ for slitting an individual's throat or exploding a building full of children, or a businessman taking credit for a five million dollar charitable donation, while the plea bargainer lifer quietly mutters his admission of _blame._ But banks manipulating the currency remain silent. And how do we onlooking citizens value these various actions ? Rather passively accept the do-ers self-valuation I would guess, giving minimal consideration to wider implications. Is the public then in the unwitting business of granting agencies licenses? Is it indifferent to actions taken in its society ? If the government has declared no law against the actors action, there is NO violation, ... only of the actor's RIGHT to express himself...so that the vigilante, the one who takes upon himself to protest, is the one in violation. Familiar modern con-tre-temps, eh ?

Responsibility, then, is a tricky business, _not_ a sure guide to undertaking or valuing actions. The bloodthirsty Arab, the business man, the lifer, and the banker can perform their actions...those actions having no detectible effect on the rest of society, because the witnessing society doesn't adopt that responsibility as individuals.

We do have group functions, laws and morality, religious and good citizenship ones, but the individual members of society are not held accountable for the acts of the miscreants, deliberately and proudly so by the democracy in the name of *freedom* and *liberty*. Only the lone citizen who takes upon himself the task of enforcement or judgment is "out of line" and called a vigilante. In such a "free" society, then, when actors are carrying out their actions without immediate consequences, the level of social propriety eventually falls to its lowest common denominator...it deteriorates.

Chinese society has existed for tens of thousands of years, in part from the structure imparted by long-lived ruling dynasties, otherwise known as famous *families*. They also honor ancestor worship. Greek "democracies" such as ours, are known for their few hundred years of shelf life. Our table of organization speaks of the "rights of individuals", nary a mention of family. Where are behavioral norms introduced and reinforced before the new citizen escapes into his world? We all know, having been through it, but we seem content to forget about it when free of it. Needless to add, but the contemporary American societal disharmony is widely acknowledged as accompanied by the "breakdown of the family". One index: murder rate in the U.S. 4-5x that of China.

Do people living as a group benefit from something between freedom and dictatorship: some degree of control? George, of course, assumed his good citizens had SELF-control. But we never required that of our new-comers. Is our prized liberty a fatal flaw, an actual attractant to scofflaws ?

ARE WE JUST PLAIN DUMB?

William S. Horowitz, M.D.
January 26, 2014

A recent book on the Moslem Brotherhood reveals that there are active functioning Sharia courts of law in Britain into which the Crown's Police are forbidden. In America there are twice as many mosques existing than on 9/11, financed and staffed by Saudi Arabia, run by The Brotherhood preaching and training their extremist philosophy.... *against the wishes of their U.S. neighbors but defended by the U.S. Department of Justice!*

They are already here (maybe for a decade) actively proselytizing their overt hatred of the "liberty" which shelters them, and we, honoring that same freedom, do nothing about it. This is only one, the latest of a long list of threats but perhaps the most serious, to the security of us and our allies, multiplying as we watch passively. It is the product of a worldly "innocence" the French call *naïveté,* which this humble observer thinks merits serious attention.

Yes, the nation is young and has lots to learn. Yes, we are a Christian tolerant nation. Yes, we are a Democratic nation with room for all. Yes, we strive for an Ideal solution to practical problems. These, and others, form our political philosophy and inform our working attitude. But the most potent may lie beyond our awareness and hence remain intractable.

In spite of numerous writings, debates, and diverse points of view expressed therein, we cannot know what lay in the hearts of George and James that helped mold that nascent body to be called America, especially not their *secret* hearts. But what can we guess, what do we *imagine?*

That in the intellectual ferment and political turmoil which comprised the invention of a brand-new self-governing society over a period of several yeas, the sought-after goal would be _PERFECTION._ I assume we can all agree that goal is unattainable. So, the product is necessarily a _phantasy,_ and a phantasy IS _UNREAL._

There, that is my thesis: that a quality of unreality has imbued the conception, organization, implementation, and conduct of our beloved country since inception, explaining, accounting for, otherwise inexplicable puzzles. For one: victorious global military presence, rescuing others, sacrificing ours, _with NO territory claimed._ Another, the election and re-election of a totally unknown mixed-breed novice lacking papers and documentation of his authenticity and legislative accomplishment but offering a celebrity-like profile suitable for idealization. Do you not see a story line or hero being acted out? These are products of imagination, not ingredients of reality, Krauthammer, trained as a psychoanalyst, should have stuck to his knitting.

WHAT DO YOU BELIEVE ?

William S. Horowitz, M.D.
February 12, 2014

As a student of human behavior my whole career, I continue to be amazed at the array of reactions to Obama's various political moves, not by any means limited to those of the masses and the intelligentsia. But even his own constituency of Negroes is beginning to fractionate.

First to note is the invention of the felicitous description "low information" voters, to encompass the largest group of his support. These comprise the truly stupid, those too busy or satisfied or elsewhere involved or non-speakers of the language, those benefitting from his generosity, up to those heartedly identified with his radical intention. They are not all stupid, except in the sense of disregarding their own survival. THAT is truly stupid and is realistically applied to ALL his support, not just those that fall for his performance, the gullible.

Then there are those who are knowing of the facts and allegations of his role as an attractive impostor, but almost bemusedly observe the drama they contentedly conclude will fail, or worry won't but are paralyzed with fear of their own (and nation's) helplessness. Included here are the "inconceivables'.

Then there are those entrusted by law and us'ns to oversee the fortunes of our nation and to remedy what needs fixin', but for the most part are merely enjoying the comforts of winning a national popularity contest's prize of largesse but make noises about their genuine concern. There are, to be sure, some congresspersons, state's governors, assorted citizens, and even public commentators aware of the threat being progressively carried out without a "smidgen" of resistance, but.... What is that *but?*

Dictators through history have managed to take control of national governments and their populations in various eras without too much trouble.... except perhaps by competing rivals.... telling us it CAN be done and HAS been done. We must dispense with the mythic protection we feel thinking "It can't happen here !" No matter the falsity in his *tin-horn* authority, he has repeatedly succeeded, even when not taken seriously. Speaking of which Obama's boldness and brashness, even of his *intentions,* speaks not of his naïveté but his very intelligent awareness of the realities of which I write. What is he so aware of?

A "nation" of millions of disparate individuals cannot readily act purposefully, even in its own defense, (though a colony of ants can) ! Thanks to our human (and its ruling philosophy) individuality. We move, even when *of one mind* with the agility of a battleship changing course.... if that fast. We are the proverbial *sitting ducks*. A collection of people respond to being told what to do like one person responds.... like the child ALL persons once were. Our first resistance to authority, our first NO at age two, is built upon, strengthened and encouraged, for the rest of development, but becomes a weakness when concerted thinking or action of the group is called for.

What do I believe? That we'll be damn lucky if the U.S.A. is saved.....I mean, YOU will be.... I'm leaving.

AN ALARM RINGING ?

William S. Horowitz, M.D.
February 26, 2014

What I and millions of others witnessed today is well worth pondering, hence: The setting was a television interview by one of the bolder "anchors" questioning one of the bolder diplomats, both well-respected for their stout defense of America. Following a stepwise inquiry into our current national policy of retrenchment, the host set up the culminating question: "Is our president deliberately setting out to weaken our country?" Avoiding the obvious inference growing out of the tenor of the colloquy, the diplomat diplomatically responded that _he_ could understand that the president and others of the "thinking class" could believe a less-formidable America could ameliorate tensions in the warring world and thus prove a benefit to it!

My jaw dropped in shock at this unexpected cave-in, leading to the following thoughts. The respondent's reply was a textbook _rationalization_ providing cover for the president and the whole administration for that matter, maybe even the whole nation, avoiding the ugly and frightening implications. Yes, _ugly and frightening,_ not to be looked at !

The common answer these days, when a TV guest expert is asked how somebody _feels_ about something, is to demur by, "Well, I'm no psychiatrist, but...". Well, _I AM a psychiatrist_ of 89 years' experience, and I say BULL! The common explanations these days for people not having the temerity to speak out about our "president" is either "Respect for the office, apathy and/or inconceivability, or fear of seeming _RACIST._ All may be operative... but imagine, when even the fully-armed policeman confronting a hidden criminal and _threatened_ by unknown force reaches for his phone to call for backup,, he wants re-enforcement behind him _because he is AFRAID !_

What's to be afraid of? He, the subject of the inquiry, is merely a non-American who has manipulated his way into the highest office in that country, has proven himself untrustworthy, has disrespected the laws of his office, and has openly bragged of his intention to transform that country into something else. And, more ominously, he is _NOT AFRAID_, openly and confidently carrying out his program.. What's to be afraid? ALL OF THAT, and THAT'S why Bolton ducked! And THAT'S what alarmed me ! He knows how the schoolyard bully becomes the adult dictator, how 19th and 20th century dictators did it and recognizes their roadmaps, he along with an unknown number of random politicos similarly silenced.. People of lesser experience and understanding, possibly a majority of our population, realize even less. Consider, even the smart and socially successful German Juden marched obligingly to their demise within all our memories.

Are **you** afraid ? We are being shown on a _platter_ our intended future. How many have that option?

WHADDYA' KNOW?

William S. Horowitz, M.D.
March 12, 2014

Every morning I awaken to open my eyes to seek out what's new, turning on the tube to find out _"THE NEWS"_, only to hear what I already heard a dozen times before. Is there no news anymore? OR, in the past when we heard less did we _KNOW_ more, and now when we hear more we _KNOW_ less?

In Colonial times we had the town crier to inform us what was happening, soon replaced by printed type, books, then a periodic Journal, then the daily newspaper, radio, television, and the internet. The _means_ of communication have multiplied over time to convey maximized amounts of information.... but do we _know_ more?

What's to know? As a conscious, sensate being we need to perceive and evaluate our environment, what exists and what is happening there, as a simple self-protective maneuver if not just curiosity. An extension of that need is the quest to learn what is _beyond_ our immediate perception, the so-called _news._

Earlier in my life-time we had esteemed purveyors of the news, _broadcasters,_ who we sought out and relied on to supply reliable information. They have been replaced by a variety of television performers variously named hosts, anchors, and personalities, who, along with a supply of pretty women with low décolletage and long, bare legs help to drawn and retain the audiences attention, often by means of 3-minute guest appearances.

Canny businessmen these hosts, many or most have taken to writing and advertising their publications on air, or hawking tickets to their live stage performances when not otherwise occupied.... in all contributing to the impression of _entertainment_, not information dispensing. Radio personalities have adopted the same recipe.

Meanwhile, the veritable century-old newspaper is steadily shrinking into non-existence.

Is THIS the acme of THE INFORMATION AGE? In earlier times those who had the thirst for knowledge could attend college or enter science, specialize in increasingly constricted fields of view in order to learn more and more about less and less. Where is the contemporary inquisitor to turn? (My wife, rock-solid, frequents the library and bookstore.) There is a profusion of so-called "*social media*" burgeoning daily to tap into, but what communication or information function they serve is entirely problematical. They, too, seem primarily entertaining. Is our civilization turning, or RE-turning, to *bread and circuses?* Sounds like the bottom of the heap, not the acme, to me.

THE ENTANGLEMENTS OF INFANCY

A case study of a modern tragedy
William S. Horowitz, M.D.
March 18, 2014

We have heard the accusation leveled at ones who mis-behave, "Why don't you *grow up?!*". Sometimes it is directed at irresponsible childishness, but some others make a specialty of It, a permanent life-long organization of personality which unfortunate observers awaken to after the rewards of human relationships have long ago passed their chance.

These people look normal, ordinary and in some cases attractive and even talented, which is why they puzzled Dr. Helene Deutsch in not being able to interact with her professional care in *Psychoanalysis*. She labeled them "As-Ifs": they happily followed the drill but *nothing happened* by way of establishing a therapeutic relationship. The writer has shared her curiosity and explored the phenomenon extensively, and this is yet a further elaboration.

The subject of this study experiences a life-long need for almost constant attention and concern from her human environment. She not only thrives on it as does the thirsty infant, but artfully *seduces* her supplier to continue the feeding when it flags. She usually has succeeded in having her target *hooked* by means of gestures of reciprocating the received *succor,* but they crumble empty of genuine content. She has no authentic concern for the giver to her, or even awareness of her benefactor's humanness, no more than a nursling has of her adult mother.

There exists a peculiar form of ambivalence toward her "object", a positive yearning and wish to please, which gives way to, not hostility, but annihilating destruction of his perception and memory, when frustrated, that he ever existed. This leads to an endless chain of disappointments in her personal, academic, and occupational pursuits. The dynamic reason for this is her strenuous refusal to permit in her supplier trust and reliance of herself, thereby refusing the assumption of responsibility for another. It is a remarkably predictable outcome of any expectations raised of her. It works equally well in the negative (see below), for "fairness or equity" were not included in her growing up, which was usually typified by pathological indulgence. (Commonly: "Spoiled").

Not observing rules, laws, and customs is typical of her "judgments", which may be ascribed to brain damage from drug abuse, which may _also_ be present. A police record may follow her miscellaneous flittings from place to place and job to job. The involved authorities are similarly disappointed in her, especially the physically attractive, bright and knowledgeable one (an "A" student) who raises hopes.

So we have an individual who wants life-long un-earned adulation, no responsibilities, and freedom to do as she pleases. Where do they arise in our society? It has been said that they occupy a significant portion of the group of young people who drop out of high school to take acting classes to become professional performers, but now-a-days one has to look no further than the Hollywood "Celebrities" who cavort on Television daily and are enthusiastically encouraged by their fans. "Oh Baby!"

The tragedy? The total waste of her valuable human capacity, and the destruction of her multiple suppliers' efforts.

LIGHTENING UP ! ! !

William S. Horowitz, M.D.
March 20, 2014

The cosmologists say (when they take time to speak to me), that the universe is expanding, infinitely, since it's brash inception. I say, nicht bei mir, buddy! I am doing everything I can to shrink _my_ world, which is tiring to keep and carry around after it has lost its relevance. Do you know what a bookcase full of a lifetime collection of treasured writings is called? _Dead Weight !_ And it's similarly true of almost everything, everything of my previous life which has lost its meaning, from the flimsiest to the gravest.

Hair, for instance, the subject of endless daily care, is cut short, unstyled, and left "natural", if not already disappearing of its own accord. Skin, likewise, is meticulously curetted of any irregularities which are not needed for everyday life. Accumulating bulges in one's contours are ignored as unworthy of unnecessary attention. No longer used rooms in one's house are shut, then abandoned for a new tighter venue altogether. Likewise with multiple vehicles (the roller skates went long ago). A bustling community of people and activities is typically relinquished with relief for a quiet out-of-the-way retreat. New, simple kitchenware takes the place of a fancy armoire of china. Preferred clothing likewise is boiled down to clean and comfortable coverings rather than those styled for exhibition.

We accumulated all these important-seeming things in the process of our expanding life in this expanding universe, but at some undesignated point in that progression _OUR_ expansion slowed and then stopped before reversing course. At that point utilitarian meanings gave way to treasured memories which ultimately milked of all meaning became the _dead weight_ taking up our shrunken _living_ spaces. So too did our near family, distant kin, best friends, inamorata, treasured activities, accomplishments, awards and punishments .... memories of all of them fading.

After which our vocabulary begins to thin, peoples' names first, then the mental calendar of time, place, and schedule of things to do. as we seek in vain for our lost physical agility. But this diminishment of our selves matches the shrunken ambit of our world, to a very evident sense of relief. We are not regretful for all we have accumulated and then discarded for it is "just life", though some of it will find value by our heirs. Nature has made it "natural" and painless, and for this gift we are most grateful.

But the greatest gift of all is to explore this unique aging experience with a companion... your spouse, child, partner, friend or fellow traveler. "Comparing notes" about new discoveries softens the surprises and what disappointments they may bring. It is the deepest shared be-ing I have ever known with another human.... don't leave home without it!

OVERTONES

William S. Horowitz, M.D.
March 26, 2014

They are the unspoken but powerful influences on our emotions and consequent behavior. They are the inferences, the implications, the hints and nuances, often more effective than the _ex_-plicit idea. They are what humans traffic in, and the stock-in-trade of the psychoanalyst. They typically are _unconscious._ This preamble is to introduce the topic discussed here, the significant part played by the _BEARD_ in human psychology and history.

The ancient Hebrews thought they were deucedly clever in co-opting the primal place in human history. "We came here first, we are the "chosen" people, we are the agents of God himself". This is the "message" however delivered. THERE, you can see the seed of reactions to come by the un-chosen. To personify their selected status, they insisted on requiring the men (who then?) to wear a full beard, and for it to remain untouched !

It came to symbolize old, alien, disguise (hidden), mysterious (dirty), authority (ultimate variety), wisdom (all-knowing and see-ing), punishing, ill-tempered (grouchy), serious and perhaps menacing (heavy), judging (of others), and, to top off these appealing attributes, writers of the law. There, nominate me for the prize, you now have the whole explanation of _anti-semitism._

I mean that seriously, for when the beard was sacrificed for clean-shaven, a whole revolutionary new era was marked, from ancient to modern, from old world to new, from biblical to contemporary, from theoretical to realistic, from Moses to Jesus.....and with that, the atmosphere of tolerance, forgiveness, love, good-fellowship and friendship, health and cleanliness. And award a double: illuminating the enthusiastic appeal and reception of Christianity.

Now-a-days we see the late-comer Moslems sporting their Spanish _half_-beards, fancy goatees of dashing but menacing mien, which are decorative but insubstantial. They are hard to take seriously, which maybe why they take pains to act ferocious. Any other commentary?

Oh, yes, the women. There we witness the full flower of human ingenuity, artistry, variety, beauty, and love of one's body in their _hairdos_, seemingly time-less down through the epochs of history. The collaborators of Vichy France were punished by having their crowning glory shaven off, quite the opposite effect of their male counterparts who were just shot, intact. (Universal ambivalence about castration ?)

Not having anything more come to mind, hair being a somewhat self-limiting subject, I'll stop now.

A COMPENDIUM OF MY PARTICULAR "HALLUCINATIONS"

William S. Horowitz, M.D.
March 29, 2014

"In case you wondered". One year ago or so, my 88th, I was made acquainted with Dr. Charles Bonnet, who 400 years ago described benign visual distortions occurring in dehydrated elderly patients who were more amused than frightened by them. Recently I was told of my esteemed senior colleague, Dr. Leo Rangell, having written a book on the same subject, his phonic. Mine made their appearance a year ago, skipped a year, now back again with a vengeance.

They come and go seemingly arbitrarily for their "cause" has yet to be identified. Recent cardiac surgery, strong drugs, advanced age and dehydration seem to be constants. They are "interesting", amusing, VERY clear, arresting of attention, and sometimes palpably cartoonish, sometimes so realistic that I am moved to interact with them, speak to or brush them away. In great profusion, they are bothersome.

I have seen a developing tiger from cub to adult luxuriating on my neighbor's tree stump, mice tunneling underground shifting mounds of dirt as they went, a multitude of human faces and heads fashioned out of foliage, brick sidings, and shaped grass and dirt collections. Three-dimensional, colored, some stable and some in realistic motion.

Inanimate objects are also caught in motion, as a sprinkler head moving down the sidewalk spraying as it went, right along a similar one holding its place in the lawn. But the most common are illusive extensions of actual objects I am perceiving or dealing with, such as the flushing toilet water appearing to fountain up at exaggerated height, or a vertically-stacked greeting card multiplying horizontally into an elongated shipping carton, or a third, then fourth duplicate of my bare feet below me..

Design patterns are common, to be seen in the air or covering random objects in the room, all or some. Simple black dots, fancy colored dots of red, green and black, triangles of the same; these do not form objects. But the most popular object is a person, 3 dimensional, clothed in colored raiment, just standing or sitting there, or in constant motion or groups including children. For some strange reason they cluster in the doorway where I'm working, often with an adult holding them back. But the most frequent occurrence is a flash glimpse of "someone" out of the "corner of my eye" before they disappear again, giving the impression my rooms are filled with people behind me.

Another mystifying phenomenon is the portrayal of simultaneous movement and not, of the _SAME_ object at the _SAME_ time (as a bus pulling away from the curb while not moving an inch). It makes me shake my head in wonderment; intellectually impossible, but there it is ! Perhaps it is done by simultaneously superimposed images.) This reminds me of protracted or repetitive imaging, _after_ shots of the same view like a defective movie reel.

My optical history is unremarkable, but I have fallen over a dozen times over two years from imbalance, striking my occiput. What starts or stops them still unknown.

EVOLUTION?

William S. Horowitz, M.D.
March 31, 2014

30,50,70.... What are they? Those are the percentages of girls in the three racial groups in our society having babies by themselves. Seems to be catching on, wouldn't you say? And we're not even shocked by it, yet. WHAT is going on?

We don't as of now have a word for it, so recent is its appearance. Is there some fundamental change in our *BIOLOGY?* Species of living creatures do go extinct, which might be signaled by a change in mating habits wouldn't you think? is it the customs of our human family that are changing...our *CULTURE or SOCIOLOGY?* Or may it be *POLITICAL*, new ways of permitted or even credited voting with the crowd, being popular, being modern?

And what do the remainder of unchanged groups think? It is *eerie* to feel the ground under you is moving, aptly called a *quake,* not knowing if it is your body, your fellow men, or some interloper selling his nostrum.

But this didn't start yesterday, or even with the invented new president. It may have made its maiden appearance somewhere in the last century or two with the development of the Industrial Revolution and humans leaving the farm, the beginning of changes the way families functioned. From time beyond memory the strong man headed, provided and protected his little society, the family. When he left home to labor in the manufactory, leaving domestic challenges to his wife, he marked a long road of retrogression to today's *option*-ality. And our making the transition from the Industrial to the Information Age, with robots appearing on the assembly line, the need for man's labor is even further marginalized.

Not only is a FATHER unneeded or wanted by those massive percentages starting half-families, but most never had one of their own. Divorce, the official sanctioning of breaking up the family, accounts for the disappearance of most once-existing fathers, not to mention the other half of the seed-providing group which never claimed their place at all. With the women suing for equal access to the workplace, plus the supply of eager one-night pinch-batters on the bench, who needs 'em, the father ?; Is he heading for extinction ? In addition, cultivating sperm could be developed into a thriving industry, and then there is always *parthenogenesis.*

Credit the lexicographers, or the masqueraders, for disguising this fundamental absence in our society. I questioned this previously in "Where Have all The Fathers Gone?". Now I have the answer: <u>legerdemain</u>. They invented the term STEP-FATHER, suggesting second or substitute, when in fact it is allowing a fantasy father to replace an actual one who is GONE. The *"step"* is nothing of the kind, as any kid familiar with him will tell (or even more malignantly, will NOT know the difference but think he had one). He is Mother's <u>*next*</u> <u>*HUSBAND,*</u> not a father to the family.

Any member of the family may be *step,* but this is where it really counts. We have to realize there is an ENORMOUS amount of father-less-ness in our world, with effects much studied and known, (e.g. juvenile delinquency), but what about that which is un-studied and un-known? Have you considered, for instance, the government, the leaders of our nation, notoriously "do nothing" "Fathers" ? What would our historic Founding Fathers, of whom we are so proud, say to today's variety? But most significantly are the multitudes of children meekly confronting their lives with a gaping hole inside, totally unaware of its source or effect, not confident, not trusting, not belonging, not happily anticipating their future. THERE'S the tragedy..

IS THAT ALL THERE IS ?

William S. Horowitz, M.D.
April 3, 2014

The plaintive cry of disappointment, Peggy Lee's reflection of the dissolute sixties, echoed the sea-change in our culture which legitimized the craving for drugs, "Something more"! "Turn on, tune in, drop Out" was the disillusioned mantra of Dr. Timothy Leary who preached the "counter-culture" from the halls of academe, yet, fathering a whole generation of "Hippies".

The fifties and Eisenhower marked the culmination of "normality" in our American culture; growth, absence of fear, and good-fellowship. The seventies marked the appearance of novel aberrations never before witnessed: flagrant sexuality in the White House, a resignation from the presidency to avoid impeachment, flaunting of homosexuality including marriage, bankruptcy of our flagship automobile industry, and recently election of a non-citizen to the presidency with a ballooning of the welfare system, to name a few.

The implication of Lee's song is something missing, lacking, not delivered, not satisfying.... as though expecting more. It is a melody of indictment of our country, of failure. American "Can't do" anymore when it used to be "Can Do !"? Once living in our society was highly desired, permitting one to aspire, to dream of what desired, then freely to achieve that.

Life itself is the gift.... "Oh, to be alive !" To bask under the blue sky, to scan the green fields, to hear the rippling brook, to receive the adoring love of your child, the kiss of your beloved, to feel content with your existence.... these are the rewards of living. What happened to them? What can determine the mood of a whole population of people, their outlook, their attitude, their hopes and fears, their *PSYCHOLOGY*? Why, it our old friend *POLITICS,* that's the word for group feel and think. And it was the politics of the dissatisfied, the un-happy, the losers that propagandized the sixties and following.

Only, the problem is the stealth of these politics, unrecognized by the naïve public, which gives them stature. They go by the name of radicals, leftists, progressives, and latterly democrats (of the people). They set up a false duality of "Liberal" and "Conservative", thereby awarding themselves legitimacy and popularity and tarring the opposition as being "old-fashioned". In actuality, the *left* is occupied by maladjusted, unhappy, envious losers, and the *right* by successful satisfied well-adjusted normals. As I have written previously, there are not two political "parties".....only one and non-one.

Most of the popular press perpetuates this deception, but Rush Limbaugh, among a very few "radio heads", explicates this puzzle excellently and intuitively (disregarding *his and all their egos*). And he remains *optimistic.* It is fascinating additionally to speculate on the possible involvement of the politics of dissatisfaction in the contemporary world-wide unrest. Once, the ideas of change, revolution, liberation from oppression carried a "good" value and were lauded by us. Now-a-days they carry the opposite, destruction of the status quo which fails to benefit the loser, a "bad", nihilistic value.

PROST

William S. Horowitz, M.D.
April 9, 2014

Yesterday I experienced a blindingly comprehensive light into my personal history and the causes of what has happened to me. It is so *total* that I despair of being able to capture it in these words, but I want to memorialize it in the only way I know. Primarily it is for me to know, but I wish it could be shared with the people involved. I'll try.

It was in looking up this Yiddish word that the insight took place. The word means *common, ordinary,* even *vulgar,* a term of deprecation. It was the realization that, in my pursuit of quality and excellence to overcome an unconscious sense of *shame, I was* the commoner I was trying to best. It was ME ! But more later.

My grades were excellent and I won honors every year at school. After medical school, I trained as a psychoanalyst (one of only 300 in the nation then). I practiced in Beverly Hills with all Hollywoodites, Palos Verdes with all physicians, serving the "cream". I presented significant scientific papers at the Institute and national congresses, and held important posts in the society, all before losing some by R's actions (below). I felt on the top.

A brief background bio is in order. I was born in the Twenties (89 now) with a 4 yr. older sister, of two old-world immigrant Jewish parents, father having lost his first wife and child, mother meeting him as a food peddler in her residence. Both were one of eight, he militantly "Americanized" in a work-a-day family, she raised in some degree of wealth and isolated by herself at her Grandmothers' after a childhood trauma. After some sojourns in 4 different cities before 5, we four settled down in a wealthy suburb away from both families, with federal help during the great Depression while my father dug ditches and my mother aspired.

Being young and naïve, I felt "like everybody else", that I *belonged*. Hence, all my friends were Gentile, to my mother's dismay, so I agreed to be "confirmed" as a Jew, but it didn't "take" at the age of 16. I deduce this has been a life-long struggle since only in recent years, after Schlomo Sands' book "The INVENTION of the Jewish Race", have I finally felt "liberated" (back to the original feeing). This was manifested in my adult life by multiple *faux pas* of knocking on doors to be told I wasn't wanted. And by the major effort, my 4 marriages.

"E" was my first, a Catholic daughter of a high-ranking military officer who introduced me to elegance with imported dishes. Our conflicted problem about having children led to failure and divorce by me. "I only want from you my maiden name back". The second was "R", the heiress of a nationally prominent Jewish industrialist (to atone for my prior "sin"?). Multiple miscarriages with consequent mis-care of our living daughter followed. It led to a protracted series of high-powered legal proceedings leading to eventual estrangement and punishing of my reputation (revenge). The elegance in this case was Jewish.

After a decade to recoup my bearings, I met "M" in a European royal setting and hastily married this Protestant woman whose mother hung out with but never married a Jewish bachelor, which experience may have "normalized" her 32 year association with this one. She was a civic social leader with political activities and aspirations.. We had one child, she refused any more, and had only marginal acceptance of my family. She died, precipitously.

My 4th marriage was to "G", after a long friendship in parallel with M. She was significantly younger, a Christian Scientist with a disarmingly simple elegance of living, willingly assuming the burden of my almost total care. I am in her complete debt and awe.

While "My People" in their arrogance looked down on non-"Members of the Tribe" as inferiors, which may have echoed in my felt need to 'atone" for E, I suddenly saw that these 4 women saw ME as prost and patiently tried to accept me.....until.....in all 4 instances......I disgusted them with my boyish "freedom". What can I say? Sorry doesn't cut it. I have been brought down to size by my realization, perhaps where I belonged before pursuing CLASS. I guess I thought that's who I was after all my "best" awards.

This leaves me thinking I'm not liberated at all. That leads to the thought of something inherited, in my DNA, in my "race"? Is Sands wrong in denying race? Is "dirty" inevitably linked to "Jew"? Is Christ and his followers "cleaning up" that identity, shaving off the beard? That would be a powerful appeal, as indeed Christianity is. That provides acceptance, removal of intolerable feelings, "saving" the subject. That means the combination of Judeo-Christian is not a duality but an evolution, from primitive to refined. How is an individual to make that progression? The believers say, "Take Jesus as your personal savior". A number of prominent Jewish-born intellectuals have done that very thing in their senium.

And can that change your "race". A study of their progeny, and/or those of other "conversos" is needed to answer that question. Meanwhile, I tried to overcome, or deny, something in me...and failed, actually inverting or reversing what I thought were the facts. That was a life-time experience, for you to ponder.

ONCE WE WERE A FAMILY

William S. and Gloria J. Horowitz
April 11, 2014

We seniors, the eldest in our generation, longingly reminisce about the television shows we *loved* to watch, regretfully no longer. These were "Homicide: Life on the Street, Borgen, Sopranos. They were compelling at the time, memorable since. What made them so?

Of course, firstly they were *quality,* undeniably, well-done script-writing and casting. Then, they were *real,* immediate, not a play to watch but a slice of actual life you could step right into. And did ! The characters were like familiar neighbors you knew by first name. And the stories *drew you in,* unlike those distractions from boredom, time-fillers or killers like daily soap operas, they were spaced to heighten your anticipation.

To the extent you were *living* the drama rather than *watching* it, certainly they served as a supplementary experience to your daily life. An *addition.* Does this suggest they filled a need, something missing? What might that be? Does the senior member of their generation lack something? Why, yes they do, living as they are in contemporary accommodations for seniors....*sans FAMILY* ! No grandparents above them, no children or grandchildren below them, a lonely stick in an only on-paper tree.

This isn't how they used to live in the old days, when they didn't know better. A family lived *together* in the same dwelling, *all the generations,* not seeing each other only once in a while.... like we do visiting our TV families? Are these powerful dramas, as well-done as they are, drawing some of that power from a contemporary social arrangement of human isolation? Is TV in general, and latest social media, filling that same gap? And did Joe Shnook pay good ducats to visit the Globe to watch King Lear for the same reason?

And my wife, an experienced woman and mother, reminds me of another factor, the power *of the story itself* in human affairs, being very aware of the universality of the child's bedtime plea: "Tell me a story". Fairy tales and Bible stories arise from love and comfort feedings by parents to little ones, never to be forgotten as learning the alphabet or potty are. That memorialization is perhaps echoed into adulthood by the appeal of classic tales presented in movies, books, and other public venues. Positive and negative alike, both testify to the persistent effect of our social heritage.

Are we solitary monkeys, not meant to be alone, missing each other?

POWER TO THE PEOPLE ?

William S. Horowitz, M.D.
April 14, 2014

We have been raised on admirable political sentiments like freedom, small government, and the above. The problem is they are failing us, increasingly resembling propaganda with populist appeal. Our current government, being ineffective and openly corrupt, is foretelling the eventual loss of that country we hold so dear, along with those esteemed principles. How does this happen?

Since history tells us this is absolutely characteristic of countries organized along "democratic" lines, which seem to have a shelf life of only 200-250 years, perhaps the failure to thrive is the product or effect of something real and unrecognized. We start the search for an answer in observing those nations with obvious staying power. They are the _dynasties,_ successively ruling families with their inherited leaders, which live for hundreds and thousands of years, for centuries!

They share two time-honored strengths, a family, and a ruler operating for his lifetime. In our lexicon, a ruler of his family, exercising his leadership continuously while alive, is called a _FATHER._ Well, what's so great about that? If you don't know, let me clue you in, _it is rare, exceedingly rare._ If there is one thing my 89 years' experience as a psychoanalyst has taught me, is that our American society is defective in that department, evidencing a high degree of fatherless-ness!.

Is it true? Believe me, I have no reason to deceive or placate you. I am not a social scientist, a newspaper editor, or a poacher of the gospel. I deal with individual people, with their life experiences, with their hearts and minds, with their missings and yearnings. My droll and creative wife has finally announced her discovery of how my "therapy" works, calling me a _"Rent-A-Daddy"._ I cannot disagree.

Men, as classically portrayed in the movies, used to be respected: "Father knows best." Now, the opposite, a jerk, a "Johnny come lately". "No-fault" easy divorce, substitute "step" fathers, father-less single young mothers (30 to 70 per cent !), Oedipus, still active after all these years, striving to dethrone him.... no end of forces to displace him. It is no wonder he is gone, in large numbers, and we "make do" without him. He is not well-represented in our general population, but also in our government as well. And we entertain the phantasy that our "Founding Fathers" and their legacy instructions are faithfully looking after us. (Disdainful sound effect now !)

I suspect that fatherlessness is not a unique United States' effect, but rather a *human one,* compelling the development of beneficial solutions like dynasties and destructive ones like dictatorships. Voting by everybody, people-power, for the best-looking volunteer is something else, and what we are going to school on these days.

GANGS

William S. Horowitz, M.D.
April 19, 2014

If you live in a metropolitan area like Los Angeles or Chicago, the mention of gang activity in your location is frightening. All you know of them is youths and adults organized in criminal activity, often illegals selling drugs for the Mexican cartels, conducting wars between those competing cartels, engaging in sophisticated financial frauds or primitive house-breaking, or wantonly assassinating innocent children in an apparent initiation ritual from a proverbial "drive-by" car. (The latter term has been adopted as a term of wanton disregard for the society while dispensing bad "cess", often said of the Press.)

These gang members, the young ones at least, come from "broken" homes or none at all, the gang constituting their entire "family". That is the polar opposite of what most of you have experienced in your teen years as absolutely normal and healthy steps in emancipation and socialization, in "growing up". Starting in junior high, often a separate school from elementary (about age 12 to 15), the teen is beginning to loosen his interests from his family to his outside school peers, with whom he wants to be *just like*. *Best friends* are found and become inseparable. After school activities are enjoyed with his new "family", in the earlier years the gender orientation is homosexual, as the process matures with age (sr. high 15 -18) the group becomes co-ed, with a half-dozen couples doing everything (but sex) together. It is here that the interest and capacity for life-long partnerships emerge, marriage culminating the process (emancipating from one's birth family, starting one's own).

In adult life we often experience (or long for in its absence) this secondary kind of family or "gang", in the university, in employment with members of your department, in the military, in fraternal organizations, in political parties....the possibilities are endless. All this testifying to our social nature, a felt-need for *like*-others.

54("*They say*"_the worst segregationists are those complaining of it being practiced against them, the Negroes, who when attending college self-separate themselves from all the other groups.) I would say from my limited perspective, the Jews run a close second.

But, there is a larger issue here. We aim for a "class-less" society, a totally fused together "melting pot", a "one from many", an un-hyphenated America. Those are our ideals, what we wish for, or rather, what George and James planned for. Is it possible, achievable, with humans for the most part raised in a FAMILY of likenesses, which we, mostly, seek out and yearn for and are relieved to find. Did our fathers not appreciate human nature? Were they too idealistic? In this process of "evening-out", (democratizing), we have achieved a very different society from all others, which some have labelled "exceptional', which also suggests superior.

Should we indict the un-American leader who aims to make us "just like everybody else"? I am getting confused: are we different or are we the same?

POSTSCRIPT TO GANGS: "OUR GANG"

William S. Horowitz, M.D.
April 20, 2014

I dedicate these essays and the correspondents with whom they are shared and discussed, YOU, who have met regularly about monthly since 1978 in varying numbers....that's 36 YEARS!

When my son Nicholas and I returned from England with two newly minted Apple II's and wrote a primitive stock charting program, the colleagues began to meet regularly at my house over investing. Soon it encompassed other interests of the group, principally motorcycle riding. We are still meeting today, usually about monthly, a smaller core group (but partially open) that is loyal to the gang. No, we don't ride anymore....but dearly wish we could!

I had a long history of gang membership, retaining close relationships with a small cadre of boy-friends and their dates from teen years now for the best part of 75 years! In the military, bored with inactivity, I joined THREE bowling leagues, and volunteered to join the OB service at night delivering babies (my record FOUR in TWO hours with saddle blocks). On the hospital staff at home, we met almost daily, the "lunch bunch" to discuss the world situation and come up with solutions.

These examples of long-lasting relationships with "my kind" are not accidental, nor incidental, to my personality, reaction to the isolation of my profession, or even the "tedium" of domestic life. I believe they illustrate and provide evidence for a felt human need to "belong" to a family, again, as I was born into. As I observed earlier, we solitary monkeys, now grown and going our separate ways, we miss each other.

This clustering of like kinds is a form of self-segregation, which superficially at least seems to conflict with the idea of disbursed sameness, _vox populi, democracy._ We are not a mob, we get lost in a mob, we are different individuals but want an association with others like ourselves. We seek gangs, neighborhoods, groups of like-minded ones, even like-looking ones. We are receptive to fixed and proven values, even idea-logues, rather than progressive, elastic, fitting all, liberal un-discriminating acceptance. Our society has lumps and we are comfortable in that. It is the reality of humans, not fake amity.

D'JA UNDERSTAND?

William S. Horowitz, M.D.
April 26, 2014

How does it happen, the world and every woman in it asks, that the prestigious World Bank president and successor to the French Premiership fornicates the hotel maid cleaning his room...and throws away his whole future in the ensuing scandal? HOW, INDEED? And human history is rife with similar examples of which there is no shortage sad to say, not merely puzzling and unfortunate but the source of un-measurable damage and pain to domestic life, wives and children. It is staggering just to contemplate the extent of the problem. Again, FOR WHAT?

What every female cannot understand (lacking his equipment) but needs to, is that this phenomenon is often psychologically without meaning, being a reflex physiological release of a built-up congestion of the gonads from persistent regular testosterone production. It is, in pure form without situational complicating admixtures, purely A RELIEF....WHEW ! What are those? A recent disruption in an on-going relationship, resentment, poor judgment, boyishness, overwhelming stimulation and opportunity (groupies with celebrities), you get the picture. These are usually minor factors, the periodic relief of pressure is the underlying permanent basis.

OF INFIDELITY, which is how the female experiences it, being *"en famile"* and _totally emotionally committed to it_ ! She feels both unloved AND betrayed, often making the misjudgment that the act had meaning, doubly hurt. This HE doesn't understand, because he didn't mean it that way. He is deeply wedded to his wife, more so than even HE knows, buried as it is in his unconscious. For the basis of his first marriage is the selection of "The woman just like the woman who married dear old Dad".

The infant and toddler boy has been characterized as having a "love affair" with the world (AND his 20 year-older mother, who

49

responds in kind). It remains a lifetime, much of the strength of it in his unconscious, signaling itself in the lyric above. On the surface is a typically boyish denial of his need for her, showing a mischievous "getting away with whatever he can" while preserving the relationship. Any mother will instantly recognize and verify this in her "boys". They remain true to her their whole lifetimes into their senium where she takes care of them once again (living long enough to do it).

NEW POLITICAL LEXICON

William S. Horowitz, M.D.
April 29. 2014

1) GROUP IDENTITY: Left, radical, liberal, progressive, socialistic, democratic, top-down, stable strong government vulnerable to dictatorship, open to all demos who have constant need to be led, juvenile, power residing in the leader who rules by *dictat*, old-world origin.

2) INDIVIDUAL IDENTITY: Right, traditional, conservative, republican, personal freedom, bottom-up self-government requiring only a limited weak national one, constant flux, unstable, adult, power residing in *vox populi* who determine their own preferences, new-world origin.

You will note the absence of any reference to "political parties" which are dubious entities to begin with, possibly a legal fiction to provide counter-balancing adversaries for argument. The author prefers a unitary theory in which there are only traditional and absence of it or anti-traditional. Astute observers have noted the absence of a coherent political philosophy by the groupies who aim to amass power by attacks on their adversaries and bald bribes to attract votes. This curiously mirrors the traditional conflicts of the young toward their elders, hence a maturational measure. Do these attitudes shift with age? Indeed they do.

Since political attitudes influence masses of humans in their activities toward themselves and their neighbors, they often determine the fate of whole nations, not to mention the effect on human civilization itself. A recent mass commentator of great respect has opted to abandon the hard sciences for the study of politics, which he regards as the most consequential knowledge to be acquired. I would emend that to be the psychological drives behind it.

It is tempting to speculate on the historic origins of the old/new-world difference in attitudes delineated here. For instance, does the former reflect easily intimidated, already frightened masses of most men who, with the exception of their leaders and explorers, were quite content with their existence? Does the advent of the new world reflect the safety and security of their geographic isolation and vast natural resources, enabling a bold revolt against constituted authority, thus warranting the description of "blessed" or "exceptional"? And if in fact in the long course of human history, we _are_ different, what does that "fact" impose on our obligations? Do we have a God-given mission to do more than petty politics?

WHA' JA' THINK ?

William S. Horowitz, M.D.
May 1, 2014

What do Jim Jones and Masada have in common? Strange confla-
tion is it? Not at all...... the connection is _MASS SUICIDE._ and any
"good Jew" would recognize it instantly, for the phenomenon is worn
as a badge of courage and pride. What entity would embrace such
a happening? The answer is a _CULT._ And what is that? It is a group
of people banded together for security under the leadership of a
"charismatic" believer in a powerful mythology promising ultimate
protection. It is easy to get in, impossible to get out: witness the current struggle in Hollywood over membership in and fealty to "The
Church of Scientology", our contemporary example.

Ever since the publication of Schlomo Sands' book about _"The
"Invention of the Jewish People",_ attention has grown about the mythology of their history, his thesis being there was NO consistent tribe
or race down through the millennia, various peoples variously adopt-
ing the religion and rejecting it at different historical times.

As a practicing psychoanalyst for well over a half-century, I am
impressed with the tenacity of the Jewish patients' hold on their
group identity, their inability to free themselves of it, compared to
the ease of movement of Catholics and Protestants into and out of
their belief systems. The modern re-entry of the Moslem sect into
our current world scene may be different and more akin to what we
are studying here.

What might have been the motivation of some ancient "rabbis"
to form a cult? Primarily it is the desire to gain POWER, power
over people, to control them, what we now call political power. How
can this be done? Firstly by inventing or amassing pieces of ancient
mythology about super-human beings or "Gods", then condemning
the subject as a sinner or malefactor, then offering him redemption by virtue of their, the rabbi's, intimate relation with the score-

keeper. It is a powerful device, so acknowledged that it was adopted by ALL the major religions. In this sense, the ancient Hebrews may well have laid down the configuration of organized religion itself.

A cult is an ultimate form of coerced group think with total loss of individual identity. It is as herding sheep. Jews should take NO solace from their high representation amongst the intellectual prize winners, for that "brilliance" does not automatically inure to them. In point of fact, the prize winner HAS LEFT THE GROUP by discovering and developing his unique interests and abilities and pursuing his specialized studies until he wins the accolade of OUT-STANDING INDIVIDUAL in his field. Marie Curie was not to be found in Church.

Furthermore, the rabbinate did no favor to their subjects, firstly by virtue of divesting them of the ability to think for themselves, as above, and then alienating them from all other people thereby engendering anti-Semitism. The command, "Do not assimilate" finally does it. To those of you who ascribe the Jews' universal condemnation to the *goyim, you have another think coming.*.

And to those of you ready to ascribe anti-Jewish sentiments to these writings, let me assure you I have as much *gemutlichkeit* as any comfortably-fed son of a *ballybuste* mother can have.

TO BE A FRIEND

William S. Horowitz, M.D.
May 13, 2014

You may regard this as natural and easy, but I propose it is a most difficult challenge, and one not automatically achieved. The reason for this is our assumption that a friendship is a duality, a pair of selves of rough equivalence. In actual fact, to _BE_ a friend requires a degree of almost self-less-ness and a degree of almost total identification with the other self. It is the _giving_ of the self to the other, entirely unilaterally, and when perceived as such by the other, reciprocated. It is an act of love.

Those fearful of giving up the self weaken or abort the unilateral process by holding back or trying to control or wrest something from the other, thus feeling intact in their self, while the other may feel "taken" by false pretense. If you are not confident enough in your self, you cannot love _or_ be a friend. Shyness, fearfulness about exposing or expressing oneself, betrays this lack of self-confidence, which doesn't permit turning away from the self to the other for fear of its disappearance. A true friend asks _nothing_ of the other, fully confident of his trust that that trust will be honored, and that "he" will not disappear in the process. The unsure one will ask for "fair" conditions in their doings; and will typically nurse a feeling of unfairness in their transactions.

Freud's invention of the technique of "free association" requires this basic trust in randomly speaking one's thoughts to another with no expectation of instant conversational "payback", plus the trust that the listener will not do one harm with their knowledge but offer something useful in time. To carry out traditional classic treatment like this for years, today, seems almost unthinkable. My, oh my, have times changed. Is this a measure of our trust of our fellow man? How does a community get things done this way? How do you repair such a world?

What does a mental health veteran have to offer to help? Try *being* a friend, in spite of your fears and hurry, extending trust and good feeling in place of worry and alarm. It will make you feel better, and may even catch on.

TESTTITLE

William S. Horowitz, M.D.
May 14, 2014

There is a war on in the field of medical management of disease, typified in the case of diabetes. It is between the authority of _numbers_ and the rhythm of _cycles._ Although the relevance of physiological cyclical variation, or _biorhythm,_ is well accepted in understanding normal processes and pharmacological influence on it, it is often ignored in favor of identifying a single point in time for an index of value in management. In diabetes, this vaunted number is the _fasting blood sugar,_ to be taken at crack of day and all calculations to be based on it. Of course, the adherents of this approach recommend taking it a minimum of four times a day (!) for "better control", as though it is a matter of supreme indifference to the punctured.

Of course compared to preserving one's life it wins hands down, but the point of this exegesis is to question the cruciality of that assumption. Numbers are easy to annotate, track, graph, and communicate, a useful shorthand to be sure. As a conveyor of really useful information about the temporal state of the disease and its management, it falls far short of the essential knowledge of the variation in the timing of the pathological element, sugar, and its antidote, insulin, for cycles move in waves or circles, harder to convey.

I for one followed dutifully for years, nay decades, determining what "my sugar" was on awakening, alternatively delighted at a level near "normal" or dumbfounded at a reading wildly out of line with what I had been doing and ingesting. leading to a matching stab at an imagined corrective dose of insulin, variety now also to be determined. The whole operation was _as hoc,_ reflecting poor control and a high chronic level of sugar. BUT, still alive at almost 90! (And most of my doctors have already retired).

SUGAR BLUES

Courtesy Gloria
William S. Horowitz, M.D.
May 14, 2014

There is a war on in the field of medical management of disease, typified in the case of diabetes. It is between the authority of _numbers_ and the rhythm of _cycles._ Although the relevance of physiological cyclical variation, or _biorhythm,_ is well accepted in understanding normal processes and pharmacological influence on it, it is often ignored in favor of identifying a single point in time for an index of value in management. In diabetes, this vaunted number is the _fasting blood sugar,_ to be taken at crack of day and all calculations to be based on it. Of course, the adherents of this approach recommend taking it a minimum of four times a day (!) for "better control", as though it is a matter of supreme indifference to the punctured.

Of course compared to preserving one's life it wins hands down, but the point of this exegesis is to question the cruciality of that assumption. Numbers are easy to annotate, track, graph, and communicate, a useful shorthand to be sure. As a conveyor of really useful information about the temporal state of the disease and its management, it falls far short of the essential knowledge of the variation in the timing of the pathological element, sugar, and its antidote, insulin, for cycles move in waves or circles, harder to convey.

I for one followed dutifully for years, nay decades, determining what "my sugar" was on awakening, alternatively delighted at a level near "normal" (WHO'S ?) or dumbfounded at a reading wildly out of line with what I had been doing and ingesting. leading to a matching stab at an imagined corrective dose of insulin, variety now also to be determined. The whole operation was _ad hoc,_ reflecting poor control and a high chronic level of sugar, BUT, still alive at almost 90! (And most of my doctors have already retired).

So, what am I in the process of trying? Getting "in phase".

1.) Taking my breakfast AND my a.m. dose of slow-acting Lantus insulin.

2.) No lunch or an apple.

3.) Taking dinner AND my p.m. dose of Lantus, yes with a small treat dessert.

I will "spot check" numbers when I think of it, keeping an eye on the experiment, but not looking to them for guidance. What do I use? HOW I FEEL, HOW MY BODY IS FUNCTIONING, BEING NORMAL. And VERY grateful.

RESPONSIBILITY

William S. Horowitz, M.D.
May 22, 2014

Our President seems to present a mystifying puzzle to our political commentators, who all acknowledge his detached, uninvolved, "leading from behind" style but simply cannot account for it. Is it his foreign Socialist orientation, is it his hidden Moslem faith, is it his quite conscious evil intent to destroy our nation? Interesting speculations to be sure but nothing more, for if they had substance (or if our Congress did) would have led to something, some action. Let us keep in mind, however, that another underlying explanation has been argued, that of _racism,_ which may merit a second look. I know, meant as prejudice, but perhaps silently revealing.

The source of his behavior is so obvious to any parent, school teacher, or miscellaneous adult, it really doesn't take a aged professional psychologist like me to offer the clue: he simply doesn't want to take the responsibility, or any for that matter. His apologists will claim he hasn't been given it, or not enough in his particular history, to have become used to it. Those of his detractors will simply point out responsibility is _taken, not given._

A digression is imperative at this point, to look at the historical facts. The Negroes came to this country as slaves, captured by Arab slavemasters and sold to our white farmers for labor, many of whom, including our Founding Fathers, released them out of revulsion long before Lincoln did. Their tribes may have been peaceable agrarians unsuited to fighting and hence captured.

The white colonists came to this country seeking political and religious freedom, crossing a formidable ocean by themselves, settling a raw country, and latterly defeating the most powerful empire on earth in a war. These two groups of men, the _tribes or races_ of them, their gene pools, their DNA, their heritages and memories were distinctly different, obviously. In ignoring that difference, in equating the two tribes as the same (human), we generate the false claim of prejudice of the rescuing and emancipating group against the other as "racism".

Obama and his ilk have been "given the opportunity to take" responsibility for themselves and their fellows similarly situated, _by_ Abraham in the Proclamation which gave them simultaneously freedom and citizenship, _by_ the American public (to the extent earned), _by_ the armed forces, _by_ the labor unions, _by_ professional sports, _by_ Wall Street, _by_ the government, _by_ the housing industry, and latterly _by_ the schools with "Affirmative Action". Our society has bent over backward to assuage its imposed and unearned "guilt" (actually compassion) in freeing Negroes to "step up to the plate" and justify their existence like everyone else, carrying their own full load of grown-up's responsibility instead of remaining wards of the white man, insisting on more! Those who have _performed_ have done well for themselves, and led the way for the rest, disproving their "racial unworthiness" imputed to the white man by the sleazy race mongers.

A whole lucrative "industry", (read social movement), has grown up from this unwanted slave history of ours, to encompass the poor, the lazy, the losers, the juveniles, and those seeking others to be responsible for them...(called the "victims"), enthusiastically endorsed by a large segment of the world's population. Since the fruits to the recipients are so rich and the rewards to the promulgators so vote-producing, it presents a formidable near-undefeatable combination. BUT, what founded and grew this great American experiment in "Power to the People", the white colonists' indomitable spirit, cannot have simply disappeared but hopefully only lost its crisis mobilization, and is awaiting a new unswallowable insult to reveal its unstoppable force.

MY "RIGHTS"!

William S. Horowitz, M.D.
May 25, 2014

The "Rights of Man", was it introduced into the lexicon around the turn of the first millennium (1066) ? How much earlier in recorded history would take a scholar or perhaps a ghost to tell us. But following its introduction, "rights" have found a revered place for themselves in our civilization. There are Jeffersonian American political rights (to the 3 L.L.P.'s), inheritance rights, property and air-space rights, copyrights, rights of succession, legal rights, rights of the accused, just to name a handful of many more. We are not short of rights. But today we hear a veritable cacophony of voices asserting that noble sentiment which has pestered our consciences since the air waves went public. I am tired of hearing that complaint, "I want my rights", as one of a spoiled child....which it closely resembles.

Aside from "Royal Privilege", self-granted by the superior beings in our human family, rights used to be earned "perks", or perquisites, that awarded a recipient a privilege for hard work, an accomplishment of merit, or an honorarium of gratitude. They were exceptional and rare. My, how our language usage has changed...nowadays they are common, nay universal, and claimed by "everyman" just for existing. And the paradoxical feature of today's variety is the absence of any related obligation on the claimant, but that traditional duty is laid on the society instead to deliver! That is you and me.

The list of rights acknowledged, and provided, by todays' open-handed government is too tedious to enumerate here, but any working taxpayer can recite chapter and verse if you need to know. The fascinating question, however, is how this came to pass here in America, not Europe, say. It seems to be a product of the creeping political philosophies of "victimology" and "multiculturalism" which has won the hearty support of every lazy bones in the whole wide world, let alone here.

Why...how? Not hard to understand: the rewards are rich, the political power to deliver it equally rewarding...an almost unbeatable combination to mulct the public until...there is no more, or somebody says _ENOUGH!_ Who might that be? How about all you naive "bleeding-heart" liberals who voted for the fraud and still respond to the high-sounding idealistic propaganda fed you. You take the credit, we pay the cost....talk about fraud! How about YOU taking responsibility for your own soft-headed error and confessing, then acting. I wonder how many churches will deliver _this_ sermon.

FEEL BETTER RX

William S. Horowitz, M.D.
May 27, 2014

Are you troubled by the gloomy outlook for your future? Have you been the target of the drumbeat propaganda of the doomsayers, the neo-Malthusians, who claim the earth is running out of space, food, clean water, clean air, people and everything else needed to sustain life? And they have the parallel claim that their environmental regulations will eliminate the dangers so that we can live happily ever after. Just vote Democratic and (they) all will be well!

I have just the REMEDY for you which I luckily came across on Book TV, CSPAN yesterday. It is an in-person book review by Robert Bryce of his "Smaller, Faster, Lighter, Denser, Cheaper" new publication exploding the lies of the doom-sayers, and documenting the optimistic actual outlook for our future. 60 minutes will cure you, and you don't even have to read the book, he says, "Just buy it !"

Don't thank *me,* believe and *do it !*

DILETTANTE

William S. Horowitz, M.D.
May 14, 2014

A gentleman of leisure, of independent means, and without obligations to anyone.

But one doesn't have to be a member of the French gentry to qualify, for we have our own home-grown variety right here in America, self- satisfied with the accommodation they have worked out with their existence. In protest of having been cheated of their just due, they seek recriminations from their family for somehow failing them, compelling continuing compassionate efforts from them and assorted others to "make it up to them". The redress of grievances is never quite finished so justifies life-long dissatisfaction and an absence of accomplishment. Actual ability plus participation in the family's legacy affords them some means, with the background assurance of more to come, so not to worry. There is thus a background complacency with a presenting frustration, the request for more.

Such people go through life without a real love (care for the other) in their history, or a real life for that matter. They typically have a scattered variety of interests which remain unfocussed and not deeply invested in, often serving the purpose of attracting others, attention getting and giving the impression of contributing something to their community. But, _giving_ is not their forte, rather rewarding themselves and seeking it from others is. They deny a real _need_ for others, having all they need and then some ("independent"), but curiously, persist in hanging around for what may be available. It's a paradox of pseudo-sociability. They resemble adults who were overindulged as children but still "didn't get enough": "spoiled".

They are unable to negotiate a genuine love relationship, remaining essentially single, even if have experimented with marriage or briefer alliances. Their relation to their own children, as parent, is problematical. They haven't finished their own childhood yet; they remain in a perpetual state "of becoming". This presents a technical problem in treating them for their work in therapy remains unfinished.

If you have taken on unwittingly such a essentially narcissistic patient, you will have him for your life-time if you permit it. The enticing trap for the therapist is their good intelligence and their presentation of plenty of intriguing material to hold his interest. They are parasitic and feed on his good will and intentions toward them.

DISCORDANCE

William and Gloria Horowitz
May 30, 2014

In the course of *evolution,* the changes that developed in the biological kingdom over prehistoric time, the great apes grew increasingly larger brains which superimposed *thinking* onto an instinctive reflexive mode of operations. The creature which resulted we call *human,* from its very beginning consisting of *two* different systems which didn't by design necessarily fit together. This is the basic origin of our concept of *conflict.* I apologize for a lexicological difficulty in referring to certain entities, for we lack names for many of these concepts!

Let's start by listing the biological instinctive preferences of the creature. The male variety is active, alone, mobile, searching, discovering, capturing, taking, possessing, guarding, competing, fighting, killing, aiming toward vanquishing and victory. The female variety is distinctively *different*, preferring passivity, waiting, receptivity, the company of others, making groups, inspirited by nature, growing living things, generating her own kind, nurturing and preserving life.

With the passage of time and intervening events, profound social changes have taken place: a _century of war_ has reduced the male population AND increased the female presence in the work place,

modern communications have introduced her to the outside world and ruptured her traditional marital bondage, the _women's' movement_ has energized and legitimized this move which, along with the _weakening of religious influence,_ has relaxed the felt strictures on all these changes.

How do these two *types* ever get and stay together in order to multiply? With difficulty, obviously, there existing an underlying discordance or *non-fit,* well before more temporal problems. So, partnering or marriage is already basically difficult and risky, and takes the surprise and shock out of separation, divorce, recriminations, rage, killing, multiple partners, avoiding altogether, or seeking safety with one's own kind. All built-in and accounted for. Our shock and awe should b reserved for accomplishers of a *Golden Jubilee* instead.

So, what should we expect for the success rate of *natural selection?* I don't know what Darwin thought, intuitive as he was, but _our_ utmost assumption that it will inure for our benefit is laughably infantile. We humans aren't and have never been guaranteed _anything_, which is why some of us don't believe anything, and others pray.

Does man have a _**better nature**_ due to his thinking? Does he have learned rules of conduct, a moral code, a conscience? Yes, and it can modify what his urges impel him. That's what civilization (of the savage in us) and religion is all about. How successful is this taming control? Very, until you lose it....so it depends. Do you go about your life sitting on the beast within you? No, you have *repressed* it (thanks, Sigmund). And so when your *fellow* "blows it", as Donne reminds us, "it blows for thee".

OEDIPUS LIVES
AMERICAN ERMINE

William S. Horowitz, M.D.
April 15, 2014

In recent papers I have raised the question of where all the fathers have gone, our society being marked by a high degree of father-less-ness. Factors adduced have included changing social norms like homosexuality, new customs both adaptive to and causative like single motherhood, built-in psychological conflicts including classic Oedipal rivalries, demographic losses from a century of wars, world-wide reproductive failure, and growth of paternalistic government replacing traditional familial support.

In addition, the author argues that our founding fathers and their legacy constitutional philosophy quite overtly provided for the political power to reside in the "people", NOT the leaders, who are to be replaced regularly so as to insure against the possible tyranny of the government, the leadership. One could say we have a son-society, not a leader or father-led nation. Accumulated political power over generations of a single family, a dynasty, is particularly abjured by our power-hoarding voters. And _ROYALTY_ is unequivalently forbidden.

So, what do we do for leadership (the traditional role of fathers)? We have our _STARS,_ our royalty. In every field of endeavor in our society, there are those whose performance excel over all others, are recognized as such, honored, followed, emulated and bowed down to.

Scientists), inventors, actors, performers, singers, financiers, dress designers, athletes.... there isn't a field without its star and its worshippers here. THAT'S where our leaders are located, NOT in the fathers of our families or nation.

So, humans have a need for following a leader, well-practiced growing up in a family, and do not relinquish it on high-aspiring rules on paper even though promulgated by esteemed "Fathers", to form their theoretically "class-less" democracy. And *that's* what propelled our current grossly mis-fit leader to his high-powered position, to lay waste all around him as any self-preoccupying King has done in the past.

To the extent that I can foresee the future yet to come, by projecting the current contretemps, I would expect this nascent "empire" to enlarge and then collapse, save for a rising revolution to overthrow it, led by *leaders* yet to emerge. From where? From strong experienced families, Mother Nature's royalty.

UN-WANTED

William S. Horowitz, M.D.
June 4, 2014

Let us explore this emotion together, for it arises so frequently in complaints about early family life experiences as to seem almost ubiquitous. Gloria asks, "Isn't this, wanting to be wanted, just the human condition?". Is such a thing possible? Can we view lovers seeking a partner who will reassure them from this pain, babies with outstretched arms begging to be held, can this really be the universal impetus for socializing?

There is the first clue, man being a social creature, wanting the company of others and wanting to be wanted by others. Humans are not alone in the biological kingdom, for many animals share this characteristic. But not all ! Leopards living in the tree and hunting prey at night for dinner, or turtles swimming in the pond to get to the other side could care less about their other kind, unless and until the rules of the jungle are suspended for the purpose of mating. Then and only then will these solitary creatures want to be wanted. Even plants, some garden people will tell you, respond to being touched.

Where does this lead or leave us? Well, even among people there are exceptions, those truly un-wanted. Some residing in orphanages for that purpose, waiting to be wanted after not, some in asylums or hospitals who are unable to make meaningful contact with their fellows, and a whole segment of society who are anti-social actors of various sorts. But all this does not clarify. We psychologists are interested in our fellows who are convinced they were not wanted by their Mother.

Does this happen in reality? Of course, and obviously. But that is rare. This emotion is not only not rare but very frequent. And the complainants adduce evidence to prove it, or remain in blithe denial in the face of it. Does this mean there is a variety of un-wantedness in many families which is reacted to and then adapted to in order to overcome the bad feeling and possibly win redemption? Are many of us carrying-on in spite of this perception/suspicion and even leading exemplary productive, non-neurotic lives? This would suggest that the emotion may be true, the source (yet to be examined) may be true, the adaptation may be true, but the symptoms or behavior or character distortions remain hidden except to the excavator. We'll leave it to your therapist to clue you in.

Can loving life-generating Mothers, right along with their ample goodies, transmit *"enough already"*? Can she experience fatigue, go off duty, "leave me alone" on occasion? We would consider her unbelievable if not. After all she is only human, and before mothering, was a happy-go-lucky young girl. So, is it possible the frequent reporting of "un-wantedness" is actual and near universal...*but forgiven and forgotten in a curative surplus of gratitude and love, not to mention idealization?*

UN-TOUCHED

William, Gloria and Kitty Horowitz
A Collaboration
June 10, 2014

As a corollary to the essay on Un-wanted, this subject arose as a related but quite separate subject, the observing of almost antiseptic isolation from human physical contact. There are simple innocuous forms such as childish shyness, more severe avoidance phobias, then outright schizoid delusional isolation. But we are considering here a widespread *cultural* form of protracted contact and its antithesis of puritanical physical isolation.

To start with its opposite, some Asian cultures boast their infants' feet never touch the ground for their first *three years,* being carried all that time. Another native culture, our own American Indian, invented the *papoose* for the same purpose. Obviously it is felt the continuous contact with the warmth of the mother's body has a beneficial effect on the infant, not to mention the bonding that must take place for her, too. Time-honored, traditional breast-feeding, a succeeding edition of the same practice, takes it's place in many, nay most, cultures and down through the ages historically. These practices have necessarily proven themselves as having useful even life-saving utility.

BUT, they are not universal, and perhaps the exceptions are illuminating. In Colonial days one group of religious refugees from the British Isles were the *Puritans,* a group of freedom seekers wanting to practice their beliefs, which included almost abstemious avoidance of habits of living and thinking which they regarded as *impure.* They formed the core of New England's emerging society and a number of succeeding Protestant sects. To a significant degree, the Puritan spirit can be found resident in America's culture yet today, not to mention Britain's.

Most of Non-American societies and politics are _socialistic,_ meaning undifferentiated mob population ruled from above. Britian's _class_ traditional society was comprised of rigidly segregated tranches of the population abjured from mixing. Winston Churchill credited his long happy marriage to his wife from NOT sharing a bed or even twins, but sleeping in _separate rooms._ The American society was _individualistic,_ on the other hand, stressing the separateness of the people, with consequent relatively rapid changes and notable instability and un-rigidity.

Evidence can be found in popular child-rearing practices. Infants are not only not routinely held close, but often not held at all, being placed in a separate room apart from the mother. { Millennial have recently revived the practice of "Jerry carriers"}. They are often left alone to cry out their unhappiness. They are most often nursed from a bottle, which may not even be held by the mother but propped up in the crib. Wealthy mothers may feel nursing is beneath them, messy, and hire a "wet nurse" to give the breast in their stead.

The process of growing up wealthy is tightly organized into supervised play, tutored schooling, careful medical evaluations, and expert developmental monitoring....in the hands of others, parents "hands off", clean. The internet has provided solitary games and "social" networks which paradoxically further isolate children from each other. Television likewise. The modern "ME" generation vs. the older 'WE the people" reflects isolation. The traditional value of _obligation,_ ties to one another, has been replaced by claims of _rights,_ individual privilege. Contemporary family life is conducted in separated generations, each alone in their own home. A puzzling developmental disorder has arisen in modern times, of apparent increasing incidence, a mixed bag of features called _Autism,_ consisting of defective sociability.

And testifying to this isolation of home-grown American life, came the development of Rosen's Bodywork (touching) _therapy_. There are a vast selections of techniques to administer to the aching body, all utilizing the "healing touch" of the human hand. Perhaps the same applies to the flowering of various psycho-therapies in general in the Western world, the popular protracted _interpersonal_ rehabilitation. (Even my particular specialty of psychoanalysis was warm, friendly and informal when introduced in Europe by Sigmund, rigidly structured and DE-personalized when imported to America.}

WHO ARE YOU NOW?

William and Gloria Horowitz
June 13 (Friday), 2014

After reviewing with my wife Gloria of the familiar language of the unhappy spouse, "You are not the same _person_ I married....fell in love with....I don't know who you are anymore", I am left wondering about everyone's _identity_. That term denotes a noun, an object, a thing, a particular _type of thing_. I am many things, e.g.: a human, a man, a married man, an American, a Californian, a retired elderly adult, a physician, etc., etc. None of these terms define my particular identity, who I am, however, the way a family name or religious affiliation or Social Security number does.

And we hunger for an identity, search for one, even pride fully boast about ours. The _value to_ somebody is representing that they _belong_ to some entity larger than just their single self, are some part of the rest of the world. So people, wanting to have more substance (than just existing in their own mind) look for groups of people they can belong to. Political parties, organized religions, civic groups, university alumni, all want your membership to swell their ranks and influence. Babbitt ("Everyman") was a compulsive joiner, the more the merrier.

But what of the good citizen who feels uncomfortable in the company of everyman, who wants to have and merits his very own singular identity? He is often located among the bright, the unique, the inventive, the famous. So, identity can be conferred by a collection of extra-ordinary traits plus _accomplishment_, or mundane everyday ones.

We mind doctors are aware of emotional conflicts over having a defined identity, so that establishing one can be problematic and never fully achieved. "The man without a country" is a poetic expression of that dilemma: he doesn't know where he belongs. Unknown or questionable parentage (e.g., single mother), adoption, divorce with step-parentage and name-change, non-resemblance to kin, geographic moves, physical change from injury or disease, changed times and circumstances, aging etc. are some of the life experiences which can produce an unstable identity. These are passively experienced, events happening *to them.*

But there are *purposely* avoided alliances, the person preferring to be unaffiliated, leaving himself nowhere in particular. My life as an example is drawing to a close, and having spent it ministering to a variety of people and their subjective inner lives while always trying to maintain neutrality (the *"blank screen"*), has left me quite unsure of my own identity.

Gloria and I have puzzled over who we are, ascribable in part to our absent fathers, but there is an existential dimension to this dilemma in addition. We agree we are not the same person we used to be. HOW can that possibly be? We are at the same time the person we are and NOT the person we were. You may say we aged, matured, or learned, but does that constitute a different, a new person? Are we one, two, or two in one?

I'll tell you a corollary: I see visual hallucinations, Dr. Bonnet variety, and one typical one is seeing a car moving and not moving simultaneously. Now, neither your priest nor rabbi nor even Sartre can elucidate THAT, but I think the mechanism has finally revealed itself: the eye's library can store images and display them to me on top of each other, in my deteriorating state. There, I've done away with religion and magic in one fell swoop! So, who am I? I still don't know. Do you?

MY CAREER AS A BALOON-BUSTER

William S. Horowitz, M.D.
June 19, 2014

I didn't choose it; it just happened. It was a natural follow-up to my boyhood bike riding to the unknown beyond, to explore and discover what was there. There was no intent involved, just an automatic activity, like breathing. If I have caused hurt on account of dashing dreams, I am sorry, truly. That is not in my bones. If I have eased or helped one's way in this difficult life, that would please me. But I am not on a mission, just going my way.

As a psycho-analyst, I aim to explore a mind and see how it works, no different than taking a watch apart to understand its works. I try to elucidate specific forces at work and their effect on the attitude or function of the person. And then to teach, educate the subject; not to hurt his feelings but to expand his understanding of himself. There is resistance to this process, but to the well-motivated patient, whatever uncomfortable emotions are loosened by the process are out-weighed by a felt relief.

What about the un-motivated subject ? We would ask, what is he doing with someone like me? There may be a variety of circumstances that would find them together, but if it was not accidental or momentary and persisted for years, one would rightfully conclude there were good reasons, even if unknown to the subject. Even if unconscious, the analyst takes it into account, knowing it must be powerful. The strongest resistances to the uncovering process are fear and shame, and have to be weakened before further work can proceed. I won't talk technique here, but to note love is a powerful healer.

It needs saying that truth-telling is a thankless job, and my "mission" is digging out reality underlying illusion, indeed the title of my book. Illusions, phantasies, make-believe are childish techniques for blunting the fearful life ahead; the grown adult is handicapped if still guiding his life with them. But if the subject insists, _c'est la vie!_ As I said, I'm not on a mission to cure the world, only to live my life.

SYMMETRY, FAIRNESS, EQUALITY

William S. Horowitz, M.D.
May 18, 2014

These are man's needs, emotional _and_ psychological, not nature's. We seek them, see them when they are not there, deny their absence, and altogether fabricate a false reality in which to operate (comfortably). You see, to acknowledge single events without a counter-vailing modulator, to admit unfairness, to see unequals...they all do the same thing, introduce risk, unpredictability, _anxiety._ This is why my pointing out the unitary nature of events in the real world goes unheeded. It is unwanted and quickly extinguished by the invention of the legalism (permitting debate) of dual competing positions.

This is a basic, fundamental truth which those of you who are interested in understanding your world and getting along in it _must_ come to grips with. There is no alternative. If you find it offensive, you may give it my name....I am proud of this discovery. Illustrative examples are almost too tiresome to mention, but I will remind you of one of the central "delusions" of false duality in our current life. (For detailed analysis, Rush has a good grasp of the idea.)

They say there are Democrats and Republicans, Liberals and Conservatives, Leftists and Rightists, Progressives and Traditionalists, and so on. In fact, there are folks who observe and honor the way things have been, and those who don't. The "anti's" attack, disparage, slur and otherwise try to discredit their opposition, but have NO alternative plan or program to offer or compete, only a juvenile wish list lacking substance. That it attracts certain-situated voters is no surprise, which of course why it was invented. Granted it yields political power, about as much as a free ice-cream does; "I'll give you my vote for another one".

Our society is rife with examples of "bending over backwards" to be fair, but you have your own memorable stories I am sure. Twenty-year prison before execution, Year-long murder trials, multiple re-trials, all in sharp contrast to the slogan about cowboys found rustling cattle, "Hang 'em high". I'm curious, what's the difference? Were the events more distant then, our feelings more fragile now, feminization of society, an increase in general anxiety.....what?

The other common, universal and effective unitary system is the one that actuates your internet. It is totally controlled in all it communicates by the presence of a single electronic signal which by its presence, or absence, can code all information possible. Powerful and simple, Nature's (reality's) way.

Earlier I had hoped our population would recover its perspective, see clearly what needed to be done, and do it, utilizing the mechanisms given us by our founders. It is still possible, certainly, but meanwhile I have been heartened by news from Australia and Holland (cf. "Go Dutch") who have made a volte-face in their public policy to correct the propaganda ("Multiculturalism") the whole world has succumbed to. They have lead the way, and we should be wise to follow their example. Hopeless has been turned to hopeful. Time to rejoice and stand UP !

CONFESSIONS OF A "PROTESTANT" JEW

William and Gloria Horowitz
March 24, 2014

I awoke late this morning, arising from a dream which portended earth-shaking meaning. I am compelled to put this down, but you needn't be impelled to read it, especially if propriety is important to you. That's my name for Protestantism.

In the dream I was in a shortened corridor of an upscale office building with 5 or 6 office doors opening from it. The wood paneling covering all was fine-grained expensively finished wood with a single initial emblem identifying the occupant. I associated a long-time friend of mine, a lawyer who has achieved prominence in local and national circles, who is a quintessential Protestant but in fact a fatherless ex-Catholic. The other persistent association was of Schlomo Sands' book "The Invention of the Jewish People", which left me feeling profoundly *liberated* as a non-stereotyped *Everyman.*

Judging by the imperative and persistent flow of ideas which have ensued in the following days, this dream is about religion. While I have not formally analyzed it, not being in that situation now, I have had associations to the graphic elements in it. For instance, the abbreviated hallway makes me think of constricted thinking, the miscellaneous doors to separately identified offices make me think of the business of organized religions, the tailored décor brings to mind the theme of Protestantism, and the portentous feeling lends importance.

My other associations were many, of my family and its two sides, my socializing experiences growing up in a rich neighborhood, and in the military, college, and medical school where I unknowingly breached the unspoken but understood barrier against people with my name. I won't elaborate details, use you own imagination, but the point of this exercise is to understand not only was I excluded repeatedly out of naïve ill-chosen approaches, but oppositely, _chosen_ ahead of my fellow-Jews because of my evident self-identification. Some would say I "passed".

My mother and her family were successful and moneyed, which is why we landed up in an upscale suburb of an industrial city while my father was on W.P.A., why all my school chums were Gentile, unbeknownst to me but a source of great regret to her, while my father's family were working-class ordinary good people but without _CLASS._

This "social" measure, a combination of looking good, prideful self-esteem, and money is the theme and metric of this essay, which I suspect is the significant motive that underlies "religious and race discrimination" in most of our societies.

Recall, it took several hundred (maybe 6) years for the early Christians to be converted from reviled and condemned to esteemed in the eyes of the Romans. And it took (maybe 1500) years for their meretricious practices to be condemned by a protesting cleric who advised "cleaning up their act", lending his name to those who felt likewise. With the still active condemnation of the Jews, it raises a interesting question: did the proclaimer's of _both_ bearded Old Testament religions induce _shame ?_

Previously I have posited that religion was a _political_ device to control people, an early expression of what we now call _propaganda._ I said it first condemned, then offered redemption, a powerful dynamic which almost universally keeps its subjects in line. I would add that today, besides the introduction of sin (badness), the scriptures work on fear and shame, which all three powerfully augment each other. Who would not respond to converting from bad to good, from fearful to courageous?

Lest you regard today's focus as picayune and of parochial concern only, this theme embodies the _espirit_ of America, the quintessential home of Protestantism, in contrast to Europe and the rest of the "third" world, largely Catholic. Much has been studied and written analyzing the complexity of human demographics, but the uniqueness of America as the "class-less" society has persisted never-the-less.

How are these forces perceived, forces not spoken about freely but certainly _felt_? The problem with sociological studies is they are conducted on the level of the observable and verifiable, accepted science. But the psychoanalysts living among us remind us of the UN-perceived, the UN-conscious, the merely FELT and moving. _THAT_ is what provides the motive and energy to immigrate, the feeling of freedom, happiness and the absence of fear, the enthusiasm and smiling face on the American.....AND, sad to say, is the TARGET of our envious, spiteful and destructive community of leftists who try to dominate us.

To the critics of my hypothesizing the Biblical Catholics were perceived as soiled, recall the revolt at the indulgences accorded the wealthy. To the critics of my identifying the Protestants as focusing on "appearances", read any American author of the thirties (cf. Sinclair Lewis's "Babbitry", et al.) One could say this first-generation Jew, in the shoes of his immigrant father who proudly wore the badge of WWI Vet and the American Legion as a hyper-patriot, proclaiming having taken in the cleaned-up "dirty Jew" image, identified with the successful suburbans around him rather than the old-world immigrants who preceded him. That was the whole idea of his father's (and his father's father) in coming here. Not surprisingly, this newer member of the reformed group could also be accused of hypocrisy, and often is by loyal orthodox Jews. To make clear, I am an equal-rejecter of _all organized religion,_ and only _look_ Protestant.

So what's to criticize, or mourn the loss of? Schlomo Sands and I join in encouraging you to celebrate the shaking off of the shackles tied on you by the bearded Rabbis, and make a similar appeal to the loyal followers of Martin Luther to finish the reform he bravely started. It is undeniable that organized religion can provide an identity (belonging). comfort (a sanctuary), and a sense of other-worldliness (spirituality). It is the _tenets_ of the system which are subject to disappointment, dis-belief, and disillusionment, some being reliable and some not, and the mythology created to express them. Have your private beliefs without the "guidance" of the Church. It's called _FREE-THINKING_!

GET A LIFE !

William S. Horowitz, M.D.
April 28, 2014

Sounds ridiculous doesn't it? How can a living creature to which this is usually addressed not have one, and where does one go to get it? But this situation is familiar enough that we recognize it, and not just with live-in brother-in-laws. It could be thought of as a kind of psychological _parasitism._ a living creature taking in and living off the external and internal life of another (admired, desired, tasty) living creature, often to its detriment by tolerating the intruder. For something _is_ taken away...and not returned.

When an infant is psychologically merged with its mother we call that _symbiosis._ In later life when the child has achieved separation of selves, a reciprocal partnership can develop between two free-standing beings, even if they are not of equivalent strength and development. A mother in her twenties can have a nurturing relationship with her progressively growing child, without loss to either. We say that _separation_ and _independence_ has been achieved.

The parasite lies in-between those developmental levels. Read on.

This is what we have been taught here in the good ole' U.S. of A. where autonomy and separate-ness are the virtues to be aspired to. We could call it the _NEW WORLD_ model of adult development. But in many parts of the globe, this "autonomy" is strongly rejected as "anti-social" or "anti-family", where the motto is as with THE THREE MUSKETEERS: _ONE FOR ALL AND ALL FOR ONE._ It is a _group identity,_ not an _individual_ one. We could call that an _OLD WORLD_ model.

How does a thoroughly foreign immigrant family to America adapt or "change their spots"?. With difficulty. A typical large Eastern European family making its way in the new land valuing, nay dependent on, family cohesion will take over the decisions and aspirations of the younger vulnerable ones with their "wisdom", producing absolutely predictable conflict. And how is this conflict manifested? By difficulty in choosing and "making a life" for themselves.

AND BY LOOKING *BOTH WAYS* at things, what we medicos label EXOPHORIA ! Yes, strong families from the old world have a problem in trying to adapt to the new ways here, and their young singing "God Bless America" at school pay the price. Can you think of a prominent public figure currently demonstrating this cultural conflict? Not so rare, eh?

It would be fascinating to trace in detail all the experiences and their effects on individuals caught in this con-tre-temps, and if I had more paper I could write for years... but it's not necessary, for these conflicted friends of ours are not dumb, and can do a more thorough job of it than I can. We, on the other hand, need to understand that when they may "cross the line" with us, they are just having "the urge to merge".

WINNING II

William S. Horowitz, M.D.
July 3, 2014

On the eve of our beloved country's 238th birthday, 12 more years to our last gasp according to many vaunted experts, it is appropriate to extend our recent insight that we are a competitive society, to our nation and its spirit. It has been captured by the encomium of _Exceptionalism,_ roundly debated and criticized by those most _envious_ of us. THAT, I believe, is the key to understanding our accomplishments as the "New World" and other nations reaction to it.

Now these concepts are modestly renamed in polite society for fear of offending, but being a psychoanalyst I suffer no such compunctions. Competing, besting, doing better than, and automatic _envy_ and denigrating and spoiling of the assertion, are stock-in-trade of _homo erectus_, as natural as going to the toilet but usually done in private.

There is no gainsaying that the Ole USA was blessed at its birth, with advantages of geographic isolation of _two_ oceans, vast natural resources of which _space_ was one, _two_ peaceful neighbors, inspiring founders carefully fashioning a _novel_ form of government, and escape from the worst political wars and conflicts of the past eras. But, starting out at the head of the race advantaged is no reason to feel obliged to even the odds. To give of our surplus, to help the less fortunate, to be good Christians, none demand we relinquish our head start and augmenting it. Contemporary mega-corporations which continue to grow to fantastic dimensions, housed here incidentally, don't.

So why do we feel guilty, embarrassed, ashamed? Because that is the _PLOY_ of the envious, to _spoil_ our good feeling which is the _spur_ to our continuing to do our best and excelling. Doing one's best and succeeding at it perpetuates it, and that is our deeply felt but perhaps privately asserted motto.

We have raised competing to an art form. What is a *handicap?* It is an imposed burden on the contestants to *even* the advantages between them so as to enhance their competition. Horse racing and golf are two examples. But dividing the contestants by class, event, league, age, and any other criteria does the same. Not only sports and games which are symbolic contests have this characteristic; academic, business, even tax laws have their classes of participants tailored to their individual strengths, with vigorous competition to best their fellows. But the most obvious of contests are those offices of government which are regularly chosen via election by the people themselves after being hotly contested. In contrast, foreign leaders inherit, win royal appointment, take office by force of arms, or otherwise accede to control without the consent of the governed. What has the attempt to do their best brought to our empowered citizens? Number One among nations, by any measure you care to address.

THAT stimulates envy in every other non-winner (*loser*) with its accompanying wish to spoil it. And those are the rest of the world, the losers who are not doing their best but just trying to survive. We are not in the big leagues, we are alone in that league and tolerating a variable and degraded record of achievement among the rest. Call me chauvinistic if you will, but I believe this is the distressing reality we are coping with.

What did you think the wars decimating the world's population were? When is the last time we declared war to "best" another nation, to win treasure or territory? Our wars have been to "help", and roundly derided by the witnessing losers. Keep that term in mind, this birthday, it explains a lot. We are The New York Yankees and rightfully proud of it.

IT FEELS SO GOOD

William S. Horowitz, M.D.
July 5th, 2014

To be proud again. Just like it used to be. Head high, spine erect, face seeking bravely forward. What it does for one's spirit, there are hardly words for it. Savor it, remember it, cherish it, it is our saving grace, and perhaps will prove to be for the rest of the misbegotten world. Am I crowing? You better believe it !

Since the advent of recorded human history, there has been so much blood, death and destruction as to overwhelm the faintest of hopes, which it has, extinguished in the souls of our fellow men. THAT'S why they merely struggle to survive with eyes glassed over to not see, why the strong and cruel and ruthless seize control of whole peoples and spare them the pain of existence, why inspired visions and ideas and accomplishments exist though they be, do _nothing_ to mollify the bad feelings which abound. Why?

Human nature. For every instance of victory, success and good fortune there exist hordes of non-winners, losers, failures, all struggling with envy and bad feelings. And we know from experience, _misery loves company._ You don't have to seek religious, political, economio, or scientific explanations for what you already know intuitively. The losers outnumber us and see to it we don't prevail.

OUR inspired forebears, so-oo un-earned as to wonder if heaven-sent, were _gentlemen_ ex-patriots from a pale believing world which they extricated themselves from _to be free_. Having won and experienced this _in-spiriting_, they devised a NOVEL form of _leadership from below_, "_by consent of the governed._" This was a veritable revolution in human history, and proved wildly successful in giving its recipients the spirit to do the best for themselves! That's all there is to it...simple, effective, respectful, honorable, dignified....GOOD!

That's your country, AMERICA (the Beautiful) !. That's not Britain from whence we were delivered, that's not France, nor Germany, Russia, Kazakhstan, nor Upper, Lower, or Middle Volta for that matter. It exists NOWHERE else in the wide world, though some are essaying trying it out. Their admiration is covered with envy and spite, aiming to de-spirit us and en-spirit themselves....but it doesn't work that way. It just tends to lump us together, eliding the differences. THIS, the distinctive and fundamental difference between THE NEW WORLD and the remainder of the map must NOT be forgotten, for it provides the possible *salvation* the preachers preach about, which will happen through our agency if it does, not theirs. It's NOT in the Almighty's hands...it's in OURS.

DICTATORS OF THE 20TH CENTURY

William S. Horowitz, M.D.
July 13, 2014

Perhaps it was the bloodiest 100 years in modern human history, with two world wars, numerous regional ones, and programs against native peoples. Stalin and Mao presided over massive populations and undoubtedly killed the most of their own. Hirohito, the emperor of Japan and its warrior class, the Samurai, cruelly raided neighbors to win *Lebensraum*. Mussolini and Castro of Italy and Cuba were client states of their big brothers. But Germany alone eventually essayed war against the *whole* world, the unlimited ambition of *their* dictator. Was it the times? The century *was* co-terminal with the end of the Aztec calendar; ask someone who *knows*.

The *star* of our line-up was born of an uncertain family tree which was officially questioned about *incest,* had an obvious *identity disorder* of not knowing where and to whom he belonged. This and the possible legacy of recessive genes, mark the initial flags of psychopathology. His early development was marked by repeated failures: he dropped out of school refusing to repeat, twice failed to win acceptance to art schools though he fancied he had talent, and had no idea what else to pursue. He functioned passably as a military messenger. But his main talent proved to be drawing audiences when he spoke in public.

After the Versailles treaty of WWI left Germany politically aggrieved, it formed a Socialist party structured around that grievance, to which our star joined for the first affiliation of his life. And he exercised his speaking ability and won recognition for it, in time becoming known and drawing audiences. Politics and swaying listeners with his passion shortly became the hallmark of his burgeoning career, which flourished as he rose in rank in the party. In progressive steps he graduated from party to national politics where he became a power in his own right. He draw a small coterie of staunch believers who became cohorts in his own party, along with forming a private police force to carry out his orders. This latter was perhaps the most effective in eventually undercutting national authority to his own. In time the Chancellor turned over the reins of the nation to him, and the rest is history.

He effectively organized a war machine and used it, he eliminated political rivals as needed, he organized a gene campaign against a whole society group eliminating millions, he executed his private police force when their work was done and they then constituted a threat, and was within a hairsbreadth of prevailing in his global war when he mistakenly over-reached to open two fronts at once... which did him in. A wild ride while it lasted, he showed his considerable talents unhampered by conscience, empathy, or sense of limits, a psychopath along with an orgy of compatriots, so suicided Alois Schickelgruber.

GETTING TO KNOW YOU GETTING TO KNOW ALL ABOUT YOU

William S. Horowitz, M.D.
July 20, 2014

It is a world of _wonder_ we are born into, and for all of infancy we are occupied in exploring and learning about it. Only with our first "NO" uttered to our Mother can we be said to have incorporated that world and become our 'self", a person, one of the objects in that world that we will hopefully continue to learn about for the remainder of our lives... until senescence sets in. At that time, a process of coming to understand who that person was begins, as though living within that person for 70 years hadn't taught us anything. We remain _innocents_ for most of our lives !

The first signals that something exists in that great unknown beyond the observable world are little aches and pains arising from previously silent parts of our own body ! Initially they respond to a little extra care, then after a while they reappear every day, and night for that matter. They are _part_ of us !

Then we notice they are different today than they were yesterday.... and we can't remember _what was_ yesterday ! Is that a relief, or another part discovered ? My, my, this self of ours is far more complicated than we ever imagined. This process of learning about ourselves for the first time (after sucking our toes in the crib) comes as something unexpected, a shock, almost like a brand-new person (old, more accurately). It makes us shake our head in disbelief, _a whole new world to fit in !_ Along that way, brand-new interests make their appearance, the first of which is beginning to assemble all we have learned about our history into an _auto-biography,_ ostensibly for our heirs, actually for ourselves.

The second novelty, actually related to the above, literally, is the urge toward nudity, the discomfort and disguise of wearing all the accumulated artifices and inhibitions of life, dispensing with them, feeling fully exposed ! Of course there is a sexual motive in this, a function long now neglected, but that is the minor key, not the major. Don't be surprised to read in the papers about _another_ Old-Timer found wandering the streets _au naturel_ ! It's natural ! Just keep your Uncle at home.

So we spent the bulk of our lives learning about the outside world, denying crowds of psychiatrists and Asian mystics gainful employment, only in the end having to do the job ourselves, to learn about us.... for it could not be avoided. My Mother's all-purpose guidance to life was, "_You'll find out_ !", with all its varied portent.

There is a problem in writing this essay, recognizing that the bare recitation of facts and sequences of events has NO explanatory value in illuminating the distinctive path a particular life took, to the subject or his reader. Why did he leave his family, or a branch of it, what enamored him of his wife which lasted a lifetime, why did he run with certain friends, what causes attracted him, what values did he teach his children, etc., etc.? The missing ingredient, hard to portray, is _quality_. One can assert it, but not necessarily thereby convey it.

One perhaps _knows_ it but cannot _claim_ it, this crucial element in decisions made and life led. _Think_ about it...that may have to do, itself sufficing to understanding yourself.

EXERCISING MY BRAIN

William S. Horowitz, M.D.
July 22, 2014

Intelligent Quotient is a number, however derived at, reflecting the _speed_ at which thinking operations can be performed, the higher the quicker. People often confuse this with _smarter,_ to which it is only tangentially related. It confers honors in academic circles, as well as a certain quality of superiority amongst the masses, or should I say by the holder toward the masses, otherwise called _contempt._ It is taught every day in school by observing those that "don't get it". This is the obverse of I.Q., we could call C.Q., the higher the lesser the _caring._ This is often the hidden side of intelligence, the attitude felt and perceived by the observers of the "one who knows". Smug self-satisfaction of childish rivalries, not useful in later life carried off the playground or classroom.

One measure of brain power is the ability to tell two from one, to _discriminate_, two points of light from one, for instance, or two similar adjectives in the language. Or two political platforms: are they essentially the same or wildly divergent? This is often deliberately obfuscated by indiscriminate language to win votes. (Among those who don't know the difference.) Although the extra-intelligent subject may be acutely aware of his speed in solving presented problems, he may be acutely _unaware_ of speaking down to his cohorts. It puzzles him his lack of social grace and the failures it generates; why, after all, he _knows !_

So, knowledge is one thing, feelings for one's fellow man is quite another... they don't come delivered in the same package. Is this why poets and political advisers alike advise _humility_ in assertions? Is this why our revered statesmen of yore are NEVER perceived as pompous.... and dime-a-dozen dictators are, regularly? Does the "School of Hard Knocks" teach humility, indulgence not? Our founding fathers, gentlemen all of patrician quality, never-the-less not only kept touch with their "lessers" but awarded "The People" the ultimate power in their wonderful invention, AMERICA. And it <u>worked</u>, never forget !

But they apparently never anticipated the necessity might arise to change the government in less than four years....their *purity or nobility* of thought ?....or tasking We the People to do the job if we are up to it ? They led the way, it's up to us to exert the effort. As Jefferson reminded us, from time to time blood will have to be shed (fight) to preserve what we have. He *knew* his fellow-men, in all their ways: THAT'S intelligence.

WHAT'S YOUR HURRY?

William S. Horowitz, M.D.
July 24, 2014

I wanted to _linger_ over my coffee
But it wasn't the smell.
It was the _dawn_
They used to call _Eos_
A Goddess to worship.

Savoring, like lingering
Is the lost art
Because it takes time.
And it feels like
We have no time,
There is so much to do!

But if we go slow
We stretch out the time,
So there is more of it
To enjoy, to live, to savor,

That's what they did on the _veranda,_
Didn't you wonder what they were doing?
They were taking their _ease_
They felt they had earned.
No recriminations about _wasting_ their time.

It was THEIR time, to savor
Or anything else they wanted.
Not obliged or owed to anyone,
Fully earned and paid for.

So, what is this huge obligation
That drives you to use up your time?
Does someone have a stopwatch on you?
And will call you lazy and wasteful?

All the wise writers of Aphorisms:
"Early to bed and early to rise
Makes a man healthy, wealthy and wise".
Ben Franklin may be the villain
Who hectored you while cavorting
In all the bedrooms in Europe.

Take heed to whom you listen,
It's not necessarily for your benefit.
You can rely on how good it feels,
To answer Nature's call to lay back
and enjoy!

ACCOMPLISHMENT

William S. Horowitz, M.D.
July 27, 2014

I guess it means *getting something done, an achievement.* I move in circles of high achievement, and most of my friends do likewise. But not all, and I am learning from them something I never realized. To successfully exist, to lead a life of one's own chosen activity or lack of it, THAT'S an accomplishment all by itself and worthy of respect. Whence cometh, after all, this drive to *DO?*

Little people and young animals are full of energy and seemed compelled to activity, random and purposeless as it may be, but necessary. Old folks are likewise compelled to in-activity. In between these poles is a normal exercise of doing, that which the subject chooses the tempo and type of. But here in our society a pressure apparently exists to get out and do, accomplish, get something done. Not only am I a practitioner of this behaviour, amongst the worst of them, but I also encourage my psychiatric patients to *make something of their life,* lest it be worthless. THIS is a BIG error of mine, only recently recognized, thanks to individuals who have *learned to live.*

So as I said, W*hence Cometh?* They tell me France doesn't have it: they minimize the work day, work week, work year, maximize the vacation time, and freely enjoy their aperitifs. No compulsion apparently to *keeping up,* with their neighbors. WE, on the other hand, are fiercely competitive, all striving to do our *best.* Makes a lot of money for our society, to be sure, and lots of winners, and losers. Does this *espirit de corps* seep into the winningest University or Sports Team and thence to our youngsters? It could hardly not.

So, French want to LIVE, Americans want to WIN. To reflect effects on health we would like to know some unfancied public health statistics comparing just the two nations: What is the total population and ratio to: longevity, divorce, cases of hypertension, household income, hard & soft liquors consumed, and homosexuality. I have no guess but need to realize the actual effects of these behaviours.

To be sure, the goad is not just competitive…there is an acknowledged moral dimension taught by our religious and elementary school teachers and a scattered few behaviour exemplars like Scout masters. And there is an obvious downside to not trying your best, of which America has its share of the world's population. But it remains *strange to uncover* something of passing value amongst the "*slackers*". So we pay token respect by admonishing, "On your way, be sure to *smell the Roses*".

ANIMALS

William S. Horowitz, M.D.
August 4, 2014

They are the ultimate realists, for they live in the _here and now_. They have no idea of death, the end of their existence. Even during the process of being captured, disabled, and then consumed, there is no anguished protest. To the observing human, it is a remarkable display of acceptance, unfamiliar to him, but he explains it to himself as, "They don't feel anything." Far, far from the truth, watching his pet bask in the sunshine and jump at a butterfly, then come to him for comforting.

We humans, higher in development in the biological kingdom, know death, and have learned to _fret_, We see how things _really are_, unlike the dumb animals, and our imagination runs riot with possibilities of other worlds and where we go after _this_ life. _There isn't any_, our furry friends are telling us, but, but, _that can't be_ ! We are deniers, they are accepters.

If you are a believer, what is He telling us with this apparent contradiction among His beloved creatures? He _could_ be saying WE are smarter, superior, deserve more out of life than pure existence, and ought to credit its source. But ask a nature lover like some I know and they will tell you His creatures, _all_ of them, rhapsodically enjoy the wonders of their existence _right here and now_ if they accept that gift.

Somehow, that's not enough for some. They want _more_ ! That's one way to understand the phantasies they construct around the bare facts of life. Perhaps we should consider ourselves lucky to have lived this life and be contented with it. We should be at peace.

WHO IS THAT STRANGER IN THE MIRROR?

William S. Horowitz, M.D.
August 6, 2014

Infant humans, like their animal counterparts before them, display what has been called "A love affair with the world", an endless fascination with what they perceive around them. They look, they listen, they touch, they play with, whatever is in their ambit, to get acquainted with their surroundings, we understand, for the purpose of adapting to it necessary for survival.

The mother that bore him and now nurtures him is recognized as the most important object in that scene and he is drawn to her and interacts with her as the center of that world with which he is in love. He has NO sense of himself, and does not exist or persist in his sensorium. There is the only "world" out there, and this provides the model of his later developed relations with them all.

All of our perceptive and manipulative capacities are oriented to the outside. Our eyes cannot look inward, nor can they distance themselves and look back at our external appearance. We loosely regard looking in the mirror as accomplishing that, but in fact there are two problems in that conception. Firstly, the "looker" is an imagined "other person", for we have no sense of self yet. And likewise, the "lookee" is not yet familiar for the same reason. All the other sensing capacities are likewise oriented externally, and it is far along in development before a sense of self emerges, into which a sensation can fit. THAT is the problem: _self_ is a late development in the human and not even proven in the animal.

We contemporary humans spend a career and a fortune to pursue the ancient's "Know Thyself"/ Whether sitting on a mountain top, hiring a personal shrink, or joining a cult, we often as not wind up in the ninth inning writing an autobiography to translate the code, knowing less and less and caring less and less as the final out approaches....never concluding that we were not designed to see inside. And our biological brethren are showing us self-knowledge is not necessary for the good life, as much as the professors preach it and the preachers profess it.

What's the point? Here's one: the subject of self-preoccupation we call Narcissism. Among characteristic behaviors, mirror-looking has top spot, named after the Greek God himself. Is he, himself, the looker, or is the subject identifying with the imagined public looking *at* him? And if his "self" is as fragile as advertised, is he really looking at a stranger? Perhaps it is truer to say the Narcissist has *no* ego than a big one, and needs to collect or construct one for healthy development. How can that be done? I know at least two ways, which I would recommend to all concerned about this problem in their social lives, friendly ones and unfriendly alike.

DO SOMETHING, accomplish something, get a sense of your agency, ability to influence. AND, get interested in ANOTHER, a mentor or love relationship will do. You will then see his regard and gratitude to you in his eyes, *now* a reliable picture of you.

FALSE REALITY?

William S. Horowitz, M.D.
August 9, 2014

A _contemporary_ (_of ours_) writer, John Kerr, has produced a book and movie called, "A Dangerous Method" about the psychoanalytic twins Freud and Jung. It reads exactly like a _contemporary_ (_of theirs_) giving authentic reportage of their activities complete with "scientific" analysis and criticism. One asks, "How does He know?"

To be sure and give him due credit, his skill at manufacturing the illusion of "AS-IF" greatly enhances the pleasure and attractiveness to the reader. THAT us not the issue. The question IS, "What need does that fulfill for our consumers in this society?" Are we so unable to handle real-reality that we want reality-like?

Contemporary observations and reports are gathered up by the traditional biographer and attributed to the source WITH-OUT including himself as one of them. Is this "modern" version progress? Or is our current appetite for _fake_ presaging something else? It must be, for the practice has invaded our press "news" reports in all media, print, T-V, and radio. It gives _immediacy, urgency, importance_ to what they produce, enhancing or _hyping_ their product. In this perspective it is another form of advertising. Nothing dire.

But since our times are so potentially catastrophic, and the reality almost unimaginable, perhaps this device serves to _obscure_ rather than _transmit_ the news. It makes it _palatable,_ which it would otherwise not be. Are we being served fake nutriment? Could this have ANY possible bearing at all on our parenting political bodies demonstrating organizational flaccid impotence? Are the media lulling us, anesthetizing us, facilitating our demise, instead of asserting their loyalty? THIS is what has bothered me listening to the various commentators all day long bewailing OTHERS' inaction. "WELL,

DO SOMETHING YOURSELF!". A current retrospective about the decade of the sixties shows the veteran deliverers of the news with all our respect and yearning revived, how it used to be. It was BETTER.

AGES, ERAS, AND MOVEMENTS

William S. Horowitz, M.D.
August 11, 2014

These are the terms we use to denote broad, sweeping changes in a whole society's thinking and practices. There have been a number of them during mans' recorded history, some recent larger examples include "The Renaissance, Industrial Revolution, Nation Building, Colonization, 20th Century Wars, The Atomic Age, Civil Rights, and by association, The Women's' Movement.

This latter arose from a small coterie of women in the last of the 20th century from a single inspiring individual, treated today as "past history" but of growing influence especially among young girls according to some. Hard to measure except anecdotally, today we attempt to speculate on exactly how influential"

IF women today were actually becoming more competitive with men according to their teaching, what would one expect to see demographically?

1) Fewer marriages?

2) Fewer children?

3) More female executives? Prisoners?

4) More divorces?

5) More single men and women? More single mothers?

6) More homosexuality?

7) More angry men committing more violence against women?

8) More war-like populations, wars and loss of men?

9) More imported labor?

10) More social instability with loss of traditional values?

11) A felt-decline in civil society, a retro-gression.

To whatever extent these speculations reverberate for you, is it worth it? Can it be stopped, reversed? Are Gloria Steinem and Betty Friedan heroes to be enshrined, or psychoanalyzed and forgotten as New York kvetchers? OR, to what extent should we wonder WHY their influence has spread? Has society REALLY denied women, and for that matter Negroes, their _RIGHTS?_ Some would argue we have _freed_ them of their traditional roles and they should be grateful ! And has the not inconsiderable damage to masculinity been totally ignored in this debate? Some would say "paternalism" had it coming?

BROTHERLY LOVE OR FRATRICIDE?

William S. Horowitz, M.D.
October 4, 2014

Our concept of the sibling *BROTHER* is Janus-faced, ambiguous and disingenuous. We have two diametrically opposite feelings about him: friendly and protective, and menacing. It has an interesting history. William Penn named his new city from the Greek for *Love and City,* coming to be known as the City of Brotherly Love, and indeed, the city itself in time earned the ironic reputation of ambiguity in its quality.

We in the regular society affectionately call our Police Big Brother for its protective function, hardly understanding why the "irregulars" regularly see him as threatening. To be out in the society free to observe what is going on, with the duty to coerce disorder and aberrant behavior explains the "menace". *They* assert it is not just a social history of misbehavior, not ever acknowledging this fact, but rather an accumulated pre-judging of them and practice of their police power. This is a major source of social unrest in our colorful neighborhoods.

There is another, quite possibly more significant problem because age-old, the family phenomenon of sibling rivalry.

This is the naturally occurring competition between children for dominance in the family and recognition by the parents. It is just one of multiple rivalries within the family members, but one of sometimes crippling effects. Because the male is stronger than his sister, his role in the rivalry is advantaged, and he can and sometimes does utilize it to the hilt. I have in mind special situations in which the brothers are so powerful by virtue of numbers, age and knowledge superiority, religious tradition, biased attitude, and any of many other factors, that the brothers don't merely beat the sisters in the race for the goal, but express their advantage with such force as to totally intimidate the girl into giving up her separate personality and aspirations to become a useless vassal of the brother. She being a girl may succumb out of love and respect in addition to fear, giving up herself in a vain adaptation.

The impetus for this article was a dramatically changed appearance and functioning of the proband discussed, exhibiting straightforward unconflicted functioning of her very good intelligence, a caring concern for others, a respectful independence from her family's expectations, and a mood of liberation or emancipation. This demonstrated to me the dynamic nature of her disability and its susceptibility to change.

Another case very familiar to me was a father in his old-world style announced his two sons would receive his full estate for his two daughters "didn't need any" for they had husbands. In time the sons played with unearned funds with unremarkable returns, while the first daughter became dean of women at a famous eastern women's college; the second daughter became dean of women at a local university.

I happen to believe this is more common than an isolated rarity, and is easily overlooked because it can conform to social expectations (of a "domesticated" wife) but results in a total loss of "woman power" in a large segment of our modern (non-agricultural) society. Even today girls are too often faced with only a handful of possibilities for a life career, which the "Women's' Movement" attempts to address by obliterating the genders.

Would you be surprised to learn Golda Meir and Margaret Hatcher *had no brothers?* Could there possibly be a few more like them in the woodwork?

THE ONE AND ONLY

William S. Horowitz, M.D.
October, 2014

How to begin? It is not easy to confess my belated discovery at my advanced age that ALL THE WOMEN IN MY LIFE WERE ONLYS, child or girl in the family, actually or functionally ! I should be an expert in describing what they have in common..(they would resent mightily this being lumped with others)..but I'm not, just your average dumb male who got into this dilemma in the first place

Am I mistaken? Maybe I am referring to a universal trait of girls, the WISH AND EXPECTATION to be the one and only? No, girls with sisters are different. They don't share all these traits. What are they?

1) The feeling of being "different" (from all the others, first felt at school). Feeling they don't "fit in", somewhat alienated, "outside", somewhat uncomfortable in a crowd, perhaps avoiding "mixing".

2) The feeling of being "special", which paradoxically has two antithetical overtones, being favored AND inadequate at the same time. The source of this is the unconscious perception of mother's ambivalence in having only one child or widely-spaced ones. This is the central source of disability, for the "chosen" one who ALSO feels she was not enough and feels GUILTY about that (if truly valued, mother would have had more).

3) The intolerance of competition when her felt-prerogatives are challenged by the presence or merely existence of "another". Not only people but others' ideas and knowledge are adamantly rejected, her understanding being the "only", rendering a profound learning disability.

4) An ignorance about the identity of the "self," often manifested by shy avoidance of self-assertion publicly, while maintaining almost grandiose expectations privately. Does a grape lying on the table

know what it is? No way to know, BUT, if it sees next to it another grape, it says, "Aha, now I know, I'm one of the bunch!"

5) Even in the presence of good or superior intelligence, an ignorance of common experience of others plus a feeling of non-entitlement, remaining deferential to others' authority and loath to exercise her own.

6) Because she feels she alone has to fill in for the missing others in being of help to her mother, she aspires to being ideally "perfect", which burden she cannot fulfill, resulting in a state of constant disappointment and failure with its mood of sadness.

7) What we are describing is an EGO DEFORMATION, a confusing mixture of opposites, confusing to the subject and observer alike. AND, to top it off, the whole picture can disappear with the subject letting herself become "regular" with others, i.e., dropping her "onliness" as a defense. But having functioned as a defense, a sanctuary from anxious interpersonal relations, it is readily retreated and clung to for "safety"

What seems to be the optimal family arrangement for healthy development ? It seems a modest number of children (4?) , both sexes, spaced by 2 or 3 years, NOT a generation apart, and two regular parents with enough resources to live decently in a community.

Being an "only" is a life-long booby prize. But, as you can tell, I loved them all.and married four of them..two of which spawned loner children as they themselves were...my last wife introduced me to genuine mothering (which I had missed) inspiring this retrospective.

PASSAGE THROUGH CYCLES

William S. Horowitz, M.D.
October 19, 2014

In the first phase of life, about five years in duration, the infant and his mother are engaged in separating themselves into two individuals from one. This process is marked by (Piaget's) first 'NO' at about 2 1/2 and is terminated by achievement of _autonomy_ (enabling attendance) at school at 5-6. During these early years, a _"self", a "me"_ is progressively formed by awareness of body parts and their distinction from others. But in memory, those experiences are fragmented and affectionately labelled the _infantile amnesia._

IF, during this passage, he is the only little one in the family, he can tell he is not his mother or his father, but he _doesn't yet know WHAT he is._ A sibling, another like him, tells him he's one of THEM, but otherwise the nature of "me" remains foggy and undefined, and can remain so FOR LIFE !

With the entrance into the world outside the family, the meeting of others, children like himself, a momentous event in the development of his "self" takes place. Firstly, an _identity_ starts to form, he is called by _name,_ not "honey or sweetheart", and he discovers in the class others exactly like himself, a _co-self_ so to speak, and they become friends ! This marks the termination of the infantile phase of development and the emancipation into the wider social world. For the only child, the process is inhibited, halting, fearful, and imperfect, a crippled relation to others. But for all the rest, friendships play a vital role in life, until, that is, this 5-yr, cycle is unwound at the other end.

During the aging phase, a not so dissimilar undoing of the infantile period takes place, with progressive relinquishment of the necessity of friends in favor of an exclusive relation with a supportive other, his spouse if fortunate, or even his pet. During this period of enclosing experience, focusing takes place, a ripening of massed memories.

With the now "empty nest" taking place of family, assorted physical and mental infirmities, memory of peak performance behind him, it takes no special insight to lead to _depression._

Which leads to NATURES self-therapy of CREATIVITY. Blossoming bursts of here-to-fore unseen expressions of inventiveness and generativity are not atypical of the aged, contrary to many expectations, lending to the life in retrospect an altogether fulsome ripening. Not to gainsay the rewards of a full life well-lived in the middle years, some say these closing ones ARE THE BEST OF THEIR LIFE !

WHO DO YOU SEE WHEN YOU SEE YOUR BELOVED?

William S. Horowitz, M.D.
November 2, 2014

Follow me in this thought exercise. It must be something other than the obvious. Let's start by assigning this adjective to it; OTHER (not me). Does that infer another person? Well, how would we know since the "other person" we differentiated from to form our very own self was another self, like us...."WE". Two pieces of me, or two me's. Long before this final separation of self took place, it could be said that we had "another self", or, ALTER EGO. This is historical FACT, not supposition.

Long AFTER the long process of physical and psychological development is completed and autonomous adulthood was attained, man being a social creature the process of RE-coupling takes place, suggesting a cycling process becomes superimposed on a longitudinal one. [Perhaps the model for future time-axes]. The "wedding" of two into one not only makes possible the RE-creation of life, but could be said to restore the original unity of selve(s). You are taking for your mate "YOUR OTHER HALF"!

IF we see in our beloved our own other self, is this a forgotten one, a wished for one, or a completed one? And IF it completes a unified "self", what happens when the seventh year arrives? Is this Mother Nature's signal of "enough?". Are romantic unions made in heaven....or just our dreams?

During infancy, the failure to couple or pair is signaled by the avoidance of eye contact or touch and is called one of the AUTISTIC groups, perhaps being increasingly recognized. But in later childhood and adulthood the distortions of ego-functioning characteristic of the only child typify the kinds of disturbances found in socialization, but not by any means restricted to them.

These also focus on the distorted "self".

But the passage of the ME through the life cycle is a tortuous and chancy affair in the extreme, rendering the (political) concept of the "individual" highly imaginary. From the mating of two humans among random millions, the selection of random genes for inheritance, the amphimixis of those first genomes into random order, the early development of a body and personality sketched above, the vicissitudes of life experience on the long and cyclical patterns, and the acquiring of mind traits by imitation, identification, ambition, adoption, and willful choice....all combine to render the self a constantly changing entity. Even the articulate autobiographer cannot transmit the full picture of his life, to his readers....let alone to his own sagging sense of self.

What is the effect of constantly changing selves in a long-term relationship? They say, "I hardly know him any more". THIS is the prototypical complaint heard in therapy offices and courts, NOT the Jubilee marriages of our grandparents, THIS is today's NORM. (What were they, then?)

We didn't recognize the shape of our Mother's left ear as that of Aunt Bessie's because we didn't know her. But she's there, with pieces of countless members of our legacy chain, forming a formless mosaic. THAT'S the nature of our legacy, and our individuality. It's true that physical and mental traits are formed into a characteristic shape which can be described in words and pictures, but it's also true that the moment you look, it has changed, again. What we see when we see our beloved, especially later...we see a stranger, familiar as he may be. Is THIS not familiar to you, spouses?

ALIENATION

William S. Horowitz, M.D.
November 18, 2014

Humans being social creatures enjoy relations with others like themselves, with two types of exceptions: the severe form of disaffection or disability manifested by averted sight or touch included in the group of AUTISMS, and the milder form of discomfort in social relations known as _ALIENATION or_ ESTRANGEMENT.

The cause of the former is still unknown but its rare appearance seemingly increasing in frequency; the cause of the latter is more common and more apparent. The subject feels not a part of, not belonging, to the social nexus around him, and vainly seeks to find a place or environment where he rightly belongs. This quest typically persists lifelong and determines many of the locations, activities, and beliefs held by him. My personal belief is that it is transmitted by identification with a mother so disturbed in her own people-relations by undue isolation, often physical.

How is the disability manifested? By the extra effort to carry out the relation: it is _difficult. tortured, not easy or smooth, episodic or staccato._ Long-term relations, like friendships or even marriages, may be broken off only to be resumed, repeatedly, with different partners yet again. Or an obvious reaction formation produces exaggerated forced displays of sociability. But the underlying feeling and motivation is _NOT BELONGING, ESTRANGEMENT._

The subject, feeling _an outsider,_ is disdainful of mass-thinking, cliches, popular sentiments and drawn to novel and original points of view, inventions, and curiosities because they are _different._ Hence they populate the innovators and the inventors, bringing a valuable contribution to human society, if even at their own personal expense of isolation.

I am tempted to analogize his situation to that of the 10% of the normal population which is _left-handed_, report also feeling different, outside, and needing to take time to translate into right-handed percepts. BUT, we may NOT be dealing with an analogy at all but the real thing. Maybe left-handers ARE the estranged in our society.... and who among you KNOW the cause of their difference?

Isn't it interesting, nay fascinating, that out of a mixed and random glob of population, a relatively constant proportion of them are different, do not fit the pattern, and have their own distinctive traits, an almost natural expression of regular reproducible non-conformity. Why and how do I know about this? Because I am one of them, the "mis-fits, or odd-balls, or regulars among the irregulars", celebrating my 90th birthday tomorrow.

I close this crucially important subject out of necessity, for I wish I had time to expand it endlessly, but I want my reading public to be aware of this constant fringe most valuable edge of our society..... They are not really odd, only DIFFERENT.

LIFE ON A FAST-MOVING TRAIN

William S. Horowitz, M.D.
December 4, 2014

THAT is one author's characterization of the blind passivity of the passenger on one's own train of life events. In this concept, one is witness, not agent, in pursuing his path. Looking back by fragmenting memories in his autobiography, he hardly knows what steered him to make the decisions he did, but the summing of events itself is an attempt to gain control or _ownership_ of that passively-experienced sequence. THIS is the task and challenge for the last chapter of his existence.

The forces that bear on an individual's choices offered to him are so multifarious, historical, diluted, modified by experience, and otherwise disguised as to be unknown to him, hence "blind" or unconscious,, hence my interest as a psychoanalyst. essentially the theater of my work. The attempt to retrospectively examine his life, "to put the pieces together", to understand it, is laudable and quite rational, but that Is not his sole aim.

I believe he wants to claim ownership of his whole life, for better or for poorer, _AS HIS......THIS IS MY LIFE!_ A final, culminating trump of the human spirit over anonymous nature.